commentaries and I am confident that this new series will continue the level of excellence that we have come to expect from him. How exciting to think that pastors, students, and laity will all be able to benefit for years to come from the wise and insightful interpretation provided by Professor Osborne in this new series. The Osborne New Testament Commentaries will be a great gift for the people of God."

—**David S. Dockery**, president, Trinity International University

"One of my most valued role models, Grant Osborne is a first-tier biblical scholar who brings to the text of Scripture a rich depth of insight that is both accessible and devotional. Grant loves Christ, loves the word, and loves the church, and those loves are embodied in this wonderful new commentary series, which I cannot recommend highly enough."

—**George H. Guthrie**, Benjamin W. Perry Professor of Bible, Union University

"Grant Osborne is ideally suited to write a series of concise commentaries on the New Testament. His exegetical and hermeneutical skills are well known, and anyone who has had the privilege of being in his classes also knows his pastoral heart and wisdom."

—**Ray Van Neste**, professor of biblical studies, director of the R.C. Ryan Center for Biblical Studies, Union University

"Grant Osborne is an eminent New Testament scholar and warm-hearted professor who loves the Word of God. Through decades of effective teaching at Trinity Evangelical Divinity School and church ministry around the world, he has demonstrated an ability to guide his readers in a careful understanding of the Bible. The volumes in this accessible commentary series help readers understand the text clearly and accurately. But they also draw us to consider the implications of the text, providing key insights on faithful application and preaching that reflect a lifetime of ministry experience. This unique combination of scholarship and practical experience makes this series an invaluable resource for all students of God's Word, and especially those who are called to preach and teach."

—**H. Wayne Johnson**, associate academic dean and associate professor of pastoral theology, Trinity Evangelical Divinity School

# 1 & 2 THESSALONIANS

*Verse by Verse*

OSBORNE · NEW TESTAMENT · COMMENTARIES

# 1 & 2 THESSALONIANS

*Verse by Verse*

GRANT R. OSBORNE

LEXHAM PRESS

*1 & 2 Thessalonians: Verse by Verse*
Osborne New Testament Commentaries

Lexham Press, 1313 Commercial St., Bellingham, WA 98225
LexhamPress.com

Print ISBN 9781683590774
Digital ISBN 9781683590781

Lexham Editorial Team: Elliot Ritzema, Danielle Thevenaz
Cover Design: Christine Christophersen
Typesetting: ProjectLuz.com

# CONTENTS

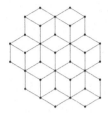

# SERIES PREFACE

There are two authors of every biblical book: the human author who penned the words, and the divine Author who revealed and inspired every word. While God did not dictate the words to the biblical writers, he did guide their minds so that they wrote their own words under the influence of the Holy Spirit. If Christians really believed what they said when they called the Bible "the word of God," a lot more would be engaged in serious Bible study. As divine revelation, the Bible deserves, indeed demands, to be studied deeply.

This means that when we study the Bible, we should not be satisfied with a cursory reading in which we insert our own meanings into the text. Instead, we must always ask what God intended to say in every passage. But Bible study should not be a tedious duty we have to perform. It is a sacred privilege and a joy. The deep meaning of any text is a buried treasure; all the riches are waiting under the surface. If we learned there was gold deep under our backyard, nothing would stop us from getting the tools we needed to dig it out. Similarly, in serious Bible study all the treasures and riches of God are waiting to be dug up for our benefit.

This series of commentaries on the New Testament is intended to supply these tools and help the Christian understand more deeply the God-intended meaning of the Bible. Each volume walks the reader verse-by-verse through a book with the goal of opening up for us what God led Matthew or Paul or John to say to their readers. My goal in this series is to make sense of the historical and literary background of these ancient works, to supply the information that will enable the modern reader to understand exactly what the biblical writers were saying to their first-century audience. I want to remove the complexity of most modern commentaries and provide an easy-to-read explanation of the text.

But it is not enough to know what the books of the New Testament meant back then; we need help in determining how each text applies to our lives today. It is one thing to see what Paul was saying his readers in Rome or Philippi, and quite another thing to see the significance of his words for us. So at key points in the commentary, I will attempt to help the reader discover areas in our modern lives that the text is addressing.

I envision three main uses for this series:

1. *Devotional Scripture reading.* Many Christians read rapidly through the Bible for devotions in a one-year program. That is extremely helpful to gain a broad overview of the Bible's story. But I strongly encourage another kind of devotional reading—namely, to study deeply a single segment of the biblical text and try to understand it. These commentaries are designed to enable that. The commentary is based on the NIV and explains the meaning of the verses, enabling the modern reader to read a few pages at a time and pray over the message.

2. *Church Bible studies.* I have written these commentaries also to serve as guides for group Bible studies. Many Bible studies today consist of people coming together and sharing what they think the text is saying. There are strengths in such an approach, but also weaknesses. The problem

is that God inspired these scriptural passages so that the church would understand and obey *what he intended the text to say*. Without some guidance into the meaning of the text, we are prone to commit heresy. At the very least, the leaders of the Bible study need to have a commentary so they can guide the discussion in the direction God intended. In my own church Bible studies, I have often had the class read a simple exposition of the text so they can all discuss the God-given message, and that is what I hope to provide here.

3. **Sermon aids.** These commentaries are also intended to help pastors faithfully exposit the text in a sermon. Busy pastors often have too little time to study complex thousand-page commentaries on biblical passages. As a result, it is easy to spend little time in Bible study and thereby to have a shallow sermon on Sunday. As I write this series, I am drawing on my own experience as a pastor and interim pastor, asking myself what I would want to include in a sermon.

Overall, my goal in these commentaries is simple: I would like them to be interesting and exciting adventures into New Testament texts. My hope is that readers will discover the riches of God that lie behind every passage in his divine word. I hope every reader will fall in love with God's word as I have and begin a similar lifelong fascination with these eternal truths!

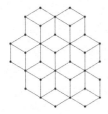

# INTRODUCTION TO
# 1 AND 2 THESSALONIANS

The Letters to the Thessalonians are often considered to be among the less important of Paul's Letters, but that is not true. They are written to a very important city with very important issues. My favorite aspect of these letters is neither the issue of the day of the Lord nor of how to handle the professional idlers but the wonderful model Paul and the Thessalonians present of a truly loving relationship between a pastor and a congregation. Throughout both letters runs a thread of respect and love that every pastor longs to experience. It provides a thrilling example of affection in extremely hard times and how that affection can make severe trials bearable.

## AUTHOR

First Thessalonians is one of those letters (with Romans, 1 and 2 Corinthians, and Galatians, called the *Hauptbriefe*, or "chief letters," of Paul) whose Pauline authorship is virtually unchallenged. He identifies himself as the author of both (1 Thess 1:1, 2:18; 2 Thess 1:1, 3:17), and both the vocabulary and the style of writing closely match the others. Moreover, the church fathers from the start accepted both as from Paul's hand (Didache 16.6; Ignatius, *Romans* 2.1, *Ephesians* 10.1). They are part of Marcion's Canon (140) and the Muratorian Canon (170), the first collections of canonical works by the early church, and are found in all the versions (Vulgate, Syriac, Old Latin).[1] So acceptance of 1 Thessalonians as from Paul is universal. However, several issues remain.

In both letters Silas and Timothy are named with Paul as authors (1 Thess 1:1; 2 Thess 1:1), and with the predominance of "we" sentences, many think Paul was merely part of a team of authors. However, there are also several "I" sentences (1 Thess 2:18; 3:5; 5:27; 2 Thess 2:5; 3:17), and it seems more likely that Silas and Timothy are co-senders rather than coauthors, and that the "we" portions are literary devices to show that the team is behind the ideas Paul is writing. So Paul is the main author.

Another issue is that some critical scholars believe 1 Thessalonians 2:13–16 to be an interpolation added later to the epistle. They think (1) the mention of "the wrath of God" that "has come upon them" must reflect a time after the destruction of Jerusalem; (2) the tone of judgment and destruction contradicts "all Israel will be saved" in Romans 11:26; and (3) the intense persecution of 2:14 did not occur as early as the writing of these epistles. However, none of the three is convincing, and there is no evidence that 1 Thessalonians ever existed without 2:13–16. The emphasis on God's judgment on the Jewish people actually stems from the Olivet Discourse on Matthew 24–25, and this in no way contradicts Romans 11:26. Paul is thinking only of unbelieving Jews here, and the idea of national revival (= "all Israel") can easily fit into what he is saying. Finally, severe Jewish persecution existed from the

---

1. Marcion was ultimately found to be a heretic, but his canon is still an important witness to second-century beliefs about the authorship of New Testament books.

start of the missionary journeys, as Acts 13–14 proves. In short, there is little reason to think 2:13–16 a late addition.

Finally, some scholars have disputed Paul's authorship of 2 Thessalonians. It was universally considered a letter of Paul in the early church and was not doubted until the nineteenth century, and even today most scholars consider it Pauline. Still, quite a few have disputed it. Let's consider their arguments briefly:

1. Its tone is apparently more formal and severe, using such later emphases as the traditions of the church (2:15; 3:6) and a tone of authoritative command, making it unlikely so soon after the warm, affectionate tone of the first letter. However, this is misleading, for Paul expresses love and affection in the second letter, and his thankfulness for them is still very evident throughout (1:3; 2:13, "we ought always to thank God for you"). When he talks discipline, he says it must be done in love "as you would a fellow believer" (3:15).

2. The **eschatology** of chapter 2 is purportedly late; some scholars argue that the "man of lawlessness" reflects the *Nero redivivus* (Nero revived) legend of the 80s and 90s, according to which Nero would come back from the dead with an army to defeat Rome. But there is no evidence for such an identification, and everything in 2:1–12 could stem from the mid-first century.

3. Others note the strong similarities between the two epistles and argue that the second letter was a near copy written by a later hand. They argue that no true author would duplicate so much material in a second letter written soon after the first. Several occur in the opening verses (1:1 = 1:1; 1:3 = 1:3–4; 1:3 = 1:11; 1:4 = 2:13), and there are several others (2:9 = 3:8; 4:1 = 3:1; 4:5 = 1:8; 5:28 = 3:18). However, this is all vastly overstated, for there are clear differences as well, such as the eschatology of the two (4:13–5:11 vs. 2:1–12) and the emphasis on "commands" in the second letter. It is much

more likely that the new sets of problems that developed just after Paul sent the first letter led to what would be typical similarities and differences between any two letters sent just weeks apart.

In short, there is little hard evidence to make us (and most commentators on these two letters) reject either as stemming from the hand of Paul.

## DATE OF WRITING AND SITUATION BEHIND THE LETTERS

It is clear that both 1 and 2 Thessalonians were written during Paul's second missionary journey, which lasted between AD 49 and 51. When we combine the details noted in these two letters with the events of Acts 17, a clear picture emerges. When Paul and Silas were asked to leave Philippi after their extraordinary prison release by God, they took the major Roman road further into Macedonia to the major city of the province, Thessalonica. There they spent a few weeks, first in the synagogues, as was their practice. They had initial success, with several Jewish conversions and even more Gentiles coming to Christ (Acts 17:1-4). However, their initial success was short-lived, as severe persecution broke out and the mission team was forced to leave Thessalonica and travel first to Berea, and then further south to Athens in the province of Achaia (Acts 17:5-10, 15-16).

Paul clearly did not want to leave Thessalonica and felt his ministry there had just begun. Both in Berea and later in Athens, he had wanted to return, "but Satan blocked our way" (1 Thess 2:18). So from Athens he sent Timothy to find out how the saints were holding up under the pressure (3:1-2). Timothy returned with very encouraging news (3:6), with the result that Paul decided to send the first letter. According to Acts 18:5 Timothy's return and thus the writing of 1 Thessalonians took place after Paul had arrived in Corinth, so about AD 50 and six months to a year after he had been forced to leave Thessalonica.

Some think 2 Thessalonians may have been written first since in that letter the persecution is a present event while in 1 Thessalonians it seems in the past; and the authenticating mark of 3:17 would fit well in a first epistle. However, there is no valid reason to think the persecution is over in 1 Thessalonians and every reason to see it as ongoing. The signature would fit just as well in a second letter as in a first. The sequence as seen in our Bibles has always been the case, and there is no reason to think we should change it. So 2 Thessalonians was written later, in AD 50 or early in AD 51.

## THE CITY OF THESSALONICA

Thessalonica was built on a natural harbor on the Aegean Sea, which gave it several trade advantages in the fourth century BC, by Cassander, a contemporary of Alexander the Great. Thus it prospered from that start, with both sea and land trade (it lay on the Via Egnatia, the major thoroughfare of the province). By Paul's time it was the largest, most populous, and wealthiest city in Macedonia.

It was also the most pro-Roman city in Macedonia, and so Rome made it the provincial capital. It was almost a second Rome, and as Rome turned more and more against Christianity, so did Thessalonica. Like Rome, they saw the emphasis on the deity of Christ as a threat to the deity of the emperor. When they supported Mark Antony and Octavian (who became Caesar Augustus), they were granted by Mark Antony the right to be a "free city." Its fame and fortune continued to grow. They built a temple to Augustus and named him and his revered uncle Julius Caesar gods. So the charges against Paul and his team were especially heinous to them.

They resembled Athens in their many gods and Roman cults. They worshipped not only the Roman gods but the Egyptian gods as well. Roman religion was amazingly pluralistic, and the average person had not only a patron god/cult they especially worshipped but countless others as well. Everyone was expected to participate in public worship observances. When Paul said in

1 Thessalonians 1:9, "you turned to God from idols," he was making a vast understatement. So when people became Christians and stopped worshipping the gods they had followed all their lives, neighbors and former friends were shocked and often angered. This was undoubtedly one of the reasons for the severe persecution they were experiencing.

## PURPOSE

Paul had several reasons for writing these letters:

(1) To encourage the Thessalonian Christians as they underwent serious opposition and severe persecution. Both the Jews and the Gentiles turned against this new religious movement, the Jews because Paul was winning many of them to Christ (Acts 17:5), and the Gentiles probably because they saw a threat in this movement that denied their gods. The two legal charges of Acts 17:6–7 reflect this, calling them worldwide troublemakers because they were a threat to the *Pax Romana*, the Roman-enforced peace that was promised to all, by their constant religious agitation. They were also guilty of proclaiming a messianic king, Jesus, and a new kingdom that would replace Rome. This plus the refusal of Christians to worship the gods who were so precious to Thessalonica brought anger down on the heads of these new converts. Paul wanted to assure them that God was on their side and that ultimate victory would be theirs.

(2) To explain to some who might have been upset at his hasty flight from Thessalonica, thinking that he had run away and deserted them. He felt a very special love for this fledgling church and was greatly impressed with their endurance and faithfulness to Christ in the midst of so much adversity. Especially in 2:1–12 he demonstrates how centered he was on their needs and how God-directed his time with them actually was. It is evident that he felt a special kinship with these people and considered them to be models of the deeply committed believer.

(3) To correct their mistaken eschatology. In the two letters there are three errors, and each caused a great deal of

consternation. First, they thought Christ was only coming for those who were still alive, so the deceased members of the church would possibly miss the resurrection of the saints. He corrects this with the official teaching (4:13-18) that at the second coming the living and the dead would be reunited and both be caught up to the Lord. Second, they were uncertain about the day of the Lord, and Paul assured them (5:1-11) that the day of judgment would catch unbelievers unawares but not them. Third, in the second epistle a false prophecy or a forged letter had convinced some that Christ had already returned and they had missed it. He countered this with the truth that before he returned the man of lawlessness would be revealed, so that day had not arrived yet. In all three Paul comforts these confused people that Christ would indeed come for them, and that they would experience vindication and victory while their persecutors would face the wrath of God.

## OUTLINES

### 1 Thessalonians

I. Introduction: thanksgiving for the Thessalonians (1:1-10)
  A. Greeting (1:1)
  B. Thanksgiving (1:2-10)
    1. The prayer and thanksgiving given for them (1:2)
    2. The basis of the thanksgiving (1:3-5)
      a. Three reasons for being thankful (1:3)
      b. The heart of the matter: chosen by God (1:4)
      c. The means of their call: the gospel (1:5)
    3. Further things for which to be thankful (1:6-10)
      a. The model behavior of the Thessalonians (1:6-7)
      b. The evangelization of the region (1:8)
      c. The story of their conversion (1:9-10)
II. The defense of proper Christian ministry (2:1-16)
  A. Original arrival: proper ministry exemplified (2:1-12)

1. Proper method for ministry (2:1-2)
2. Proper motive for ministry (2:3-4)
3. Distancing themselves from popular speakers (2:5-8)
   a. Three disclaimers (2:5-6a)
   b. Choosing the path of humility (2:6b-7a)
   c. Choosing the path of caring and sharing (2:7b-8)
4. The past care the team bestowed (2:9-12)
   a. Their intense labor (2:9)
   b. Their fatherly care (2:10-12)

B. Their reception of Paul's team: imitation through suffering (2:13-16)
   1. Accepting the words as the word of God (2:13)
   2. Imitating the suffering churches of Judea (2:14)
   3. Identifying the persecutors (2:15-16)
      a. Their evil actions (2:15a)
      b. The kind of people they are (2:15b-16a)
      c. The divine judgment they are facing (2:16b)

III. Paul's desire to see them again (2:17-3:13)
   A. His deep longing to be with them (2:17-20)
      1. Efforts to see them (2:17)
      2. Satan's obstacles (2:18)
      3. Paul's glory and joy (2:19-20)
   B. Timothy's mission to them (3:1-5)
      1. Timothy sent to strengthen them (3:1-2)
      2. The danger that persecution brings (3:3-4)
      3. The reason for sending Timothy (3:5)
   C. Timothy returns with good news (3:6-10)
      1. Good news about their continuing affection (3:6)
      2. Good news about their firm stance in Christ (3:7-8)
      3. His great joy and desire to see them (3:9-10)
   D. Concluding prayer (3:11-13)
      1. For their return to the Thessalonians (3:11)

  2. For the strengthening of their love and their hearts (3:12–13)

IV. Moral and ethical instruction (4:1–5:22)

 A. Live so as to please God (4:1–2)

 B. Sanctification means avoiding sexual immorality (4:3–8)

  1. Thesis: God demands holiness in sexual practices (4:3)

  2. Three attendant commands (4:4–6a)

  3. The coming judgment of Christ (4:6b)

  4. Concluding thoughts (4:7–8)

 C. Love and solitude in the church (4:9–12)

  1. Love for one another in the church (4:9–10)

  2. The need for self-sufficient Christians in the church (4:11–12)

 D. Confusion over the future of the dead at Christ's return (4:13–18)

  1. Thesis: correcting their ignorance about the future of the deceased (4:13)

  2. The anchor for their hope: Christian belief (4:14)

  3. The teaching of Jesus on the issue (4:15–17)

   a. The fate of those who are alive (4:15)

   b. The place of the dead at the second coming (4:16)

   c. The place of the living with the dead at the second coming (4:17)

  4. The purpose: encouragement (4:18)

 E. Getting ready for the day of the Lord (5:1–11)

  1. Sudden destruction at the day of the Lord (5:1–3)

   a. Its unexpected nature (5:1–2)

   b. Its mode: sudden destruction (5:3)

  2. Contrasts between the believer (light) and the unbeliever (darkness) (5:4–8)

   a. Believers as the children of light (5:4–5)

F.  Final greetings (3:16–18)
    1.  Peace benediction (3:16a)
    2.  Prayer of encouragement (3:16b)
    3.  Personal greeting with autograph (3:17)
    4.  Closing benediction (3:18)

## THEOLOGICAL THEMES OF THE THESSALONIAN LETTERS

**The doctrine of Christ:** Paul presents Christ distinctly as the exalted Lord, ruler of all and the king who will return to claim his people and anchor his victory over evil. The title that predominates above all is *kyrios*, appearing forty-five times, nearly always showing the exalted status of Christ as Lord over creation. In a world that centered on the divinity of the emperor and demanded that its citizens participate in the worship of the gods, the Thessalonians desperately needed to be aware of the lordship of Christ. So nearly every reference to Christ reminds them of his control over creation, a life "inspired by hope in our Lord Jesus Christ" (1 Thess 1:3). When they are especially beleaguered in fairly constant persecution, they need to realize anew that these enemies will be "shut out from the presence of the Lord ... on the day he comes" (2 Thess 1:9–10) and that the ultimate victory will be theirs.

**The gospel:** Paul emphasizes in these letters that response to the gospel produces salvation. In 1 Thessalonians this message of eternal hope is filled with power from the Holy Spirit (1:5), and in the midst of suffering it produces joy (1:6) and triumphs over opposition (2:2). Paul's successful proclamation of the gospel led to this model of a church (2:8–9) that serves as an example of triumphant Christianity all over the world.

**Eschatology:** The Lord's Prayer has as one of its themes the cry, "your kingdom come" (Matt 6:10), and one of the earliest cries of the church was "Marana Tha" ("O Lord, come" in 1 Cor 16:22). Paul's teaching in these letters on the return of Christ is thus precious to every Christian, for this tells us our future. Let us look at each of the three points in turn:

1. The resurrection of the saints: In 1 Thessalonians 4:13–18, he answers the questions of when and how we will begin our eternal future. At the **parousia** (coming) of Christ, three things will take place. First, the bodies of the dead in Christ will rise from the grave (from 2 Cor 5 we know our spirits will be with Christ); second, these deceased will be united with the living saints who are caught up from earth; and third, they both will receive their glorified resurrection bodies when together they "meet the Lord in the air" (v. 17).

2. The day of the Lord: In 1 Thessalonians 5:1–11 and 2 Thessalonians 1:7–10 Paul carefully explains the second aspect of Christ's return. For believers the parousia means reunion with deceased saints and reception of the glorified body. For unbelievers it means judgment and eternal punishment. They are appointed for wrath (1 Thess 5:9) and payback for sins (everlasting destruction) on the day he comes (2 Thess 1:9–10).

3. The revelation of the man of lawlessness: In 2 Thessalonians 2:1–12, the final event in human history, in a sense inaugurating the return of Christ, will be the coming of the absolute antithesis of Christ: the antichrist, or man of lawlessness, who will be the personification of Satan, the final attempt of the cosmic powers of evil to wrest victory from the hand of God and destroy his people once and for all. This will take place when God's control over this world, which has "restrained" evil, is removed, and for a short time these evil powers will be allowed to operate. But this time is to be short-lived, and the doom of this figure, as of all evil in this world, is assured.

# 1 THESSALONIANS

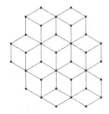

# INTRODUCTION: THANKSGIVING FOR THE THESSALONIANS
### (1:1–10)

P aul employs the traditional opening style of **Hellenistic** let-ter-writing in all his letters, beginning with the author(s) and proceeding to the recipients, concluding with the greeting itself. However, this is one of the briefer and simpler openings, for Paul does not add any further descriptions of himself (like "apostle of Christ Jesus") or of the recipients (like "to the saints in ..."). The greeting is simple as well, probably because he has been there in the recent past. It is also true that while he is deeply concerned for the Thessalonians since he was forced to leave before he had time to anchor them in the Christian truths, he is quite pleased with their commitment to the Lord and their endurance in the midst of intense persecution. He does not need to stress his apos-tolic authority, as they already fully accept that.

## PAUL GREETS THE THESSALONIAN BELIEVERS (1:1)

He names Silas (Silvanus in the Greek) and Timothy as coauthors or senders of the epistle. The addition of these names does not mean they had cowritten the letter but that they were in com-plete agreement with it and were part of Paul's team that was

sending it. They were with Paul when the gospel was brought to
Thessalonica and the church was established there. Paul is writing this from Corinth after Timothy arrived from Thessalonica
with the news Paul was waiting for. It was very good news indeed
regarding their faithfulness and firm stance in the Lord (3:6, 8;
Acts 18:5), so the two associates are also involved in this epistle.
Still, the uses of the first-person singular "I" in 2:18; 3:5; and 5:27
indicate Paul alone and make it likely they supplied information
but did not participate in the actual writing of the letter. The use
of "we" in the letter is Paul showing how the entire mission team
was involved in the ministry to the Thessalonians. He adds their
names to acknowledge their critical contributions to this church.
They launched this church and were instrumental in its successful growth thus far.

Silas (the Jewish form; Silvanus is the Greco-Roman form of the
same name) was a leader in the Jerusalem church chosen to deliver
the decision of the Jerusalem council to Antioch (Acts 15:22, 27),
and Paul asked him to join his team (Acts 15:40). Many believe that
when Paul and Barnabas split (Acts 15:39), Silas took his place as
coleader of the mission team, and this may explain why his name
appears before Timothy's here. He remained at Corinth after the
second missionary journey, perhaps to help right that church after
all the difficulties there. Later, he became an associate of Peter
and in 1 Peter 5:12 is the **amanuensis**, or secretary, who pens that
letter on behalf of Peter.

We must remember that Timothy was a very young man at this
time and joined the team from his hometown of Lystra (Acts 16:1–3),
the product of a Jewish mother (his father was a Greek unbeliever)
and a faithful grandmother (2 Tim 1:5). He became a virtual son
to Paul, who trusted him enough to make him his ambassador
or representative and sent him often on important missions to
strengthen churches (Acts 19:22; 1 Cor 4:17; Phil 2:19; 1 Thess 3:2–6).
Later he became Paul's emissary to Ephesus and then their virtual pastor (1 Tim).

Paul is sending the letter to all the believers in Thessalonica and calls them a "church" (*ekklēsia*), a term that to them normally designated the "assembly" or council of citizens that ran the city. It likely has two connotations here: first, the assembly of the citizens of heaven, those designated the people of God and called to belong to him. Second, they are in continuity with the covenant people of Israel and form the Gentile component of the new Israel, the church of God.

He further designates them as assembled "in God the Father and the Lord Jesus Christ." The "in" (*en*) has a double meaning and signifies that God is both the sphere ("in") and the means ("by") of the church's existence. They are distinguished from the political or social assembly, for they belong to God and the Lord Jesus. It has come about not by human effort or socioeconomic forces (not even of Paul and his team) but entirely by an act of God. Moreover, the source of it all is the fatherhood of God and the lordship of Christ. We are the family of God and the servants of our Lord at one and the same time. Ours is a privilege and a power that intertwine in producing an eternal force—we are the church of Christ as well as the children of God.

The greeting is also simpler than usual but still profound. Paul combines the Greek greeting *charis* ("grace") and the Hebrew greeting *shalom* ("peace"). As greetings they were metaphors expressing the respective hopes that the recipients would experience a gracious and peaceful life. Paul is filling the terms with theological depth and saying in effect, "What you merely hope for is now being offered to you in fullness by God and Christ." The unmerited grace and mercy of God and the life of wholeness and peace that it brings now become a reality in Christ.

## PAUL GIVES THANKS TO GOD FOR THE THESSALONIAN CHURCH (1:2-10)

In the vast majority of Paul's letters the greeting is followed by a prayer and a thanksgiving for what God is doing among them.

Here these are combined into a single section as he expresses his joy at the victorious life they are living. At the same time, it has been proved that the introductory thanksgivings usually contain a prelude of the contents of the letter, providing a preview of the themes to come. This is true here as well. He celebrates the coming of the gospel and the conversion of the Thessalonian believers (vv. 4–5), their faithful endurance in persecution (v. 6), the model they have become for other churches (vv. 7–8), and the victorious life that resulted from their conversion (vv. 9–10).

### The Prayer and Thanksgiving Given for Them (1:2)

This is letter-writing convention, as most letters in the first century contained a brief declaration of thanksgiving for the recipient. Yet Paul always went way beyond the conventional, turning the thanks into a brief essay preparing the readers for the contents of the letter. Paul is expressing the constant thankfulness he offers to God on their behalf ("We always thank God for all of you"). This becomes a frequent refrain; the encouraging report of Timothy after Paul's months of worry waiting for news (3:2–6) led him to rejoice greatly at all God had done for them. In this section his joy is generated by the story of their conversion and subsequent growth in Christ. Every time Paul thought of them he gave thanks, for everything resulted from God's involvement in their lives.

Paul had been forced to leave them too soon (2:17) and was filled with anxiety for these recent converts who were not ready to be left on their own. We should remember that the team had gone to Athens not originally to minister but were waiting for news (Acts 17:16). So when it finally came with Timothy, the worry gave way to rejoicing and thanksgiving. The statement here ("always thank God for all of you and continually mention you in our prayers") is not a formula statement or mere formality but expresses his actual feelings and practice. This is true also of the expansive "for all of you," which means he is praying not only for those who have successfully grown spiritually but also for those beaten down by circumstances (for instance, the persecution of v. 6). His prayers for them are comprehensive and ongoing, seen in both the corporate prayers of the team and Paul's personal prayer life.

## THE BASIS OF THE THANKSGIVING (1:3-5)

### Three reasons for being thankful (1:3)

As Paul and the team are praying for the newest church, they "remember" what God has done for them. This is a major biblical term, connoting not only what God brings to their mind but also the action it produced. Memory in Scripture always leads to reaction and spurs people to action. Here the team is remembering the three spiritual results of their conversion, all of them expressed by genitival ("of") phrases surrounding the three classic Christian virtues (faith, hope, and love) found together so often in Paul (1 Thess 5:8; 1 Cor 13:13; Gal 5:5-6; Eph 4:2-5; Col 1:4-5) and elsewhere (1 Pet 1:21-22; Heb 10:22-24):

1.  *The work of faith*: This is what is called a "subjective genitive,"[1] where faith is active, resulting in the NIV, "work produced by faith." This combines the vertical (faith in God) and the horizontal (good works) dimensions of the Christian life. There is an important difference in Paul between the plural works (the works of the law) and the singular work (working for God). The work Paul envisages here is holistic, combing evangelistic work with the works of the victorious Christian life. The presence of "faith" proves it is not the works of the law in Paul's mind (faith versus works) but is rather the "good works" of the Christian life that are the

---

1. When the governing noun has a verbal idea ("work"), we ask whether the genitive is subjective (active), faith doing its work, or objective (passive), faith receiving the work. Clearly here it is an active faith that is envisaged.

result of a life of faith. Their new faith in Christ has led to their working on behalf of Christ.

2.  *The labor of love*: This is also a subjective genitive, "labor prompted by love." It is very close in meaning to the first, as "labor" and "work" are synonyms, though *kopos* ("labor") is slightly stronger, designating hard work. Love has prompted strenuous activity on their part for the benefit of those around. Galatians 6:10 provides a good summary of the meaning of this work: "let us do good to all people, especially to those who belong to the family of believers." In this context the "love" is especially focused on fellow believers, as in 1 Peter 1:22: "sincere love for each other," so that you "love one another deeply, from the heart." In this letter Paul develops the theme of the Thessalonians' love for each other in 3:11–12 and 4:9–12, where he urges them to have a love that will "increase and overflow … for each another" (3:12). Their deep brotherly love has led to vigorous labor for the benefit of their fellow believers.

3.  *Steadfastness of hope*: As the other two above, Paul stresses Christian hope as inspiring and producing steadfast endurance in the midst of the troubles and trials of life. Probably Paul has the persecution of verse 6 (also 2:14–15; 3:1–5) especially in mind. In the midst of strong opposition and great pressure placed on them by outsiders, they persevered and flourished, and the reason they were able to triumph over terrible adversity was their hope in Jesus. There is a strong emphasis in both epistles on the **eschatological** future when Christ returns and God destroys this world of evil (1:10; 2:19; 3:13; 4:14–17; 5:2–3, 23). That knowledge gave them a concrete hope in the certainty that they would share Christ's triumph over evil, and that enabled them to endure the present sufferings. Hope for the world is ephemeral and uncertain, with no anchor in reality. Hope for the believer

is certain and firm, anchored in the reality of the risen Lord and his lordship over this world.

### The heart of the matter: chosen by God (1:4)

In verse 3 Paul grounded his thanksgiving in the Christian virtues that constituted their character in the Lord. The godly nature of their virtuous conduct is what enables him to "know" or be assured that they are in fact the chosen ones. So here in verse 4 he anchors this godly character in the central basis of it all—the fact that they are the elect of God. They are known for their love (v. 3), and that love is itself grounded in the fact that they are "loved by God." The horizontal love for each other stems entirely from the vertical, the fact that God loves them and has chosen them to be his.

He is indeed "God and Father" (v. 3), and that fatherly love transforms his children into loving people. Paul, in fact, labels them "brothers and sisters loved by God," for they are now part of his family, beloved children of God and siblings of one another. Paul's emphasis here is on the double bond that unites these saints—a bond with God their loving Father, and a bond with one another as brothers and sisters. In the Old Testament this was the covenantal nature of the relationship between God and his people. It was not like the pagan gods, with adherents trying to placate and win the love of the gods. It was the opposite, a matter of God's love and his initiation of a covenantal relationship with them.

The truth is, they did not offer sacrifices to purchase or win God's favor. He chose them, and they became the "elect," the chosen people. In these two letters Paul uses adelphoi ("brothers") twenty-eight times, and love dominates both letters. The brotherly love of the saints for one another develops out of the fatherly love of the Godhead, and they are part of a new social matrix, the family or brotherhood of believers. They have been estranged from this world, but they have been embraced by God and by the members of their new family. There is not only a spiritual or theological side of the concept of election, but a social side as well. God's people

are now part of an eternal "society," the church. Paul is emphasizing God's choice rather than ours. He has made us his own and
freely accepted us as his children. We could not do it on our own;
he has done it for us and adopted us as his family (Rom 8:14–17).

*The means of their call: the gospel (1:5)*

God elected them, but it was the call of the gospel that worked it
out in their lives. He chose them and then sent Paul and the mission team to proclaim the gospel to them. The gospel then came
with double strength—both the words of the gospel itself and the
power of the Spirit behind it. Once again, the vertical (the call
of God and power of the Spirit) and the horizontal (the proclamation of the gospel) go hand in glove. Paul can know why (*hoti*,
"because")[2] they are indeed the elect of God: they have responded
to the powerful gospel that came to them via the Holy Spirit.

Note that the content of the message is not only "the gospel of
God" (2:8) but also "our gospel" because God revealed it to Paul and
his team, making them his chosen heralds to proclaim the "good
news" to the Thessalonians. This introduces one of the primary
themes of this epistle, preparing for his lengthy presentation in
2:1–16 of his ministry to these people. Many scholars and writers
have noted the use of *euangelion* ("gospel") in the Greco-Roman
world for the "good news" about the emperor and his edicts. Here
the ultimate Lord of all is giving his message of hope and salvation,
not a temporary braggadocio of mere human claims but eternal
truths about the Master over all.

So unlike the proclamations of the Roman power machine,
this good news came to them "not simply with words [like the
Romans] but also with power, with the Holy Spirit and deep

---

2. Some translate this as "that" rather than "because" and understand it as
explanatory, further defining what Paul "knew," namely their election and
their conversion. However, the emphasis here is not on the fact of their conversion but the results, showing how Paul knew they were indeed chosen by God.

conviction." Let's take these three terms defining how the gospel came to the Thessalonians—words, power, and deep conviction—one at a time:

1. "With words": "with words" and "power" are not in contrast to one another but are interdependent, with the words of the proclamation undergirded with power. There is almost a double meaning—the words of the Word. The gospel must be proclaimed by the human herald, and the words are obviously critical. Every day I write this commentary, I am praying that the Spirit will fill me anew (Eph 5:18). I am not inspired in the same way Paul was, but I can be illuminated and led in what I write by the Spirit. My prayer is that I write what the Spirit leads me to say so as to inspire Bible studies and believers who can be inspired by the meaning and power of these verses. The words I choose are clearly critical, but the power comes from the Spirit. In 1 Corinthians 2:4 Paul states it very well: "My message and my preaching were not with wise and persuasive words, but with a demonstration of the Spirit's power." Still, the words chosen by the preacher are critical and become the medium through which the Spirit works.

2. "With power": It is possible that the power of the Holy Spirit includes not only the words of proclamation but also the miracles that in the early church often came with the proclamation (called "power" in Mark 6:5; Acts 14:3; Heb 2:4). Paul's main emphasis, though, is upon the Spirit's using the preaching of the gospel to change lives and convert lost souls (as in Acts 1:8; 5:23; 1 Cor 2:4-5). The power refers primarily to the mighty truths conquering the deceptive lies of the world and their power to change lives.

3. "Deep conviction": The first two are the means by which the gospel goes forth, and this third concept describes the results of the gospel. While on the surface it seems that this would refer to the convicting power of the word in

the lives of the Thessalonian converts, the word Paul uses here, *plērophoria*, means "full conviction" but also has the idea of "fullness." As such it likely applies more to the conviction of Paul and his mission team, who are convinced of the power of the gospel. So most commentators prefer this latter view—these preachers of the gospel are convinced of the power of the Spirit behind their proclamation and see it at work among the Thessalonians.

The rest of the verse appeals to the evidence these people have provided to the effective power of Paul's ministry—"You know how we lived among you for your sake." The high moral character of Paul and his associates confirms the quality and power of the gospel. He will appeal to their own awareness of this several more times (2:1–2, 5, 11; 3:3–4; 4:2). Not only the message but also the life of the messengers witnessed to the true value of God's truths for their lives. So they could trust what they were being told. Nothing Paul did was to enhance his image or money purse. It was all for their benefit and theirs alone.

## FURTHER THINGS FOR WHICH TO BE THANKFUL (1:6–10)

Here Paul returns to the theme of verse 3, the exemplary Christian lives they are living.

### The model behavior of the Thessalonians (1:6–7)

The depth of the faith, love, and hope of these saints was evident to all, as they imitated the examples of Paul and the other leaders (v. 6) and then in turn became models for other churches to emulate (v. 7). First, this celebrates the extent to which they internalized and then practiced what they were being taught: "You became imitators of us and of the Lord." In verse 5 Paul told how the gospel had come to them, and now we are told how they received that Spirit-empowered message. The depth of the response fitted the depth of the proclamation.

Note the two-way street of imitation, beginning with their imitation of Paul's team and the Lord, and proceeding to their function as a model that others imitate. This is the path of discipleship seen also in 2 Timothy 2:2: "the things you have heard me say ... entrust to reliable people who will also be qualified to teach others." Both spiritual truths and the Christian lifestyle that results are meant to be passed on to others. To fail to do so is to be a failure in God's eyes, as in Hebrews 5:12: "by this time you ought to be teachers [but instead] you need someone to teach you the elementary truths of God's word all over again."

Imitation is the core of discipleship and has two aspects to it, calling for a model life that is worth copying and for reception and obedience to the spiritual qualities demanded by their teaching (see 1 Thess 2:14; 2 Thess 3:7, 9; 1 Cor 4:16; Phil 3:17; Gal 4:12). The church needs constant concrete examples to follow. Some have accused Paul of a self-centered desire for authority over others in this, but we must begin with 1 Corinthians 11:1, "Follow my example, as I follow the example of Christ." Note the stages, as Paul builds his life around Christ and then asks the Thessalonians to observe his concrete example of the Christ-filled life. This is not ego but disciple-making. Here as well imitating Paul and the others is actually a step to imitating the Lord more fully.

A major theme throughout the two letters is the experience of suffering and persecution these Christ followers have had to pass through. So in the second half of verse 6 Paul says, "you welcomed the message in the midst of severe suffering." As both Christ and Paul had experienced severe opposition and rejection, so too had the Thessalonians. In fact, this was characteristic of the original evangelization of these believers, as in 2:2, "with the help of our God we dared to tell you his gospel in the face of strong opposition." The violent and hostile response of the pagans to the success of the gospel in Thessalonica was both immediate and severe. The likelihood of such suffering was actually part of Christian instruction (Acts 14:22, "We must go through many hardships to enter the kingdom of God"), as Paul often told them (3:3–4).

Some interpreters have understood "severe suffering" as mental anguish and anxiety rather than actual persecution, but that is quite unlikely. Persecution is a major theme in both letters, and it must mean extreme opposition and not just internal distress. In 2:2 Paul tells them about his difficult experience of persecution in Philippi (Acts 16:19–40), and that must be part of this verse as well.

They did not just endure the opposition. Paul says they even "received the word" (NIV "welcomed the message") with joy in spite of great suffering. Their very conversion was accompanied by great hardship, and yet their joy in the Spirit overcame that. This is remarkable! Severe persecution came hard on the heels of their newfound faith, and they were still overjoyed with it. That does not seem possible, and normally it would not be so, but the key is that their rejoicing was the result of the presence of the Holy Spirit in them.

The attitude of the early church to suffering was one of privilege and joy. The theme is called the "messianic woes": God has established a certain amount of suffering his Messiah and followers would have to endure, and when it was complete the end would come. So Paul could say of his own suffering, "I fill up in my flesh what is lacking in regard to Christ's afflictions" (Col 1:24). This means that our own suffering is a "participation in his sufferings" (Phil 3:10), a sharing of Christ's afflictions, and filling up what remains leading up to the end of history (also Rev 6:11).

So the Thessalonians rejoiced at the part they were allowed to play in the messianic sufferings of Christ and his church, the messianic community (Matt 5:11–12; Luke 21:28; Acts 5:41; 2 Cor 7:4; Jas 1:2–4; 1 Pet 1:6–7). This joy hardly stemmed from the situation but from the Holy Spirit. Those suffering for the Lord realized that God would repay and that the final victory was certain. Joy does not always mean happiness, for hardship is always "painful" and yet in the Spirit produces "a harvest of righteousness and peace" (Heb 12:11).

In verse 7 their incredibly mature reaction to persecution and the joyful response it occasioned resulted ("and so") in their becoming "a model to all the believers in Macedonia and Achaia." This was natural for Macedonia, for Thessalonica was the chief city of that province, but Achaia (southern Greece, containing Corinth and Athens) shows how well-known they had become in the Christian world. The term for "model" (*typos*) pictures an exact pattern or mold used to reproduce a figure or object. It says in effect that they had become a blueprint for other churches to emulate, a pattern of victorious Christian living for others to copy. They had imitated the Lord and Paul and now had become models for others to pattern themselves after. Paul's strategy was to establish churches in the leading cities of a region and trust them to evangelize their regions (Rom 15:19), and Thessalonica had become a model city for that approach, as all of Macedonia and even Achaia was reached by them (the topic of v. 8 below).

*The evangelization of the region (1:8)*

Paul is thankful not only for their implicit witness by their exemplary reception of the gospel and reaction to persecution but also for the explicit evangelistic activity they embarked on in their region. They fulfilled Paul's strategy (see previous paragraph) perfectly as "the Lord's message rang out from you not only in Macedonia and Achaia." This is the second area in which they have put into practice what they received from Paul and his team—first the joyous response to suffering (v. 6) and now the proclamation of the gospel in mission.

Paul highlights two aspects of their evangelistic activity: (1) "The Lord's message" is interpreted by most subjectively as "the word of the Lord," emphasizing not the content of the gospel message but its source—the Lord has given it to the church. It has "rung out" from them, a strong verb meaning that it has exploded forth like thunder or a trumpet blast, and the power of the message has been heard everywhere. This outstanding church boldly took the gospel everywhere in the peninsula, both to northern Greece (Macedonia) and the south (Achaia).

(2) Their "faith in God has become known everywhere." The first aspect of their evangelism was direct witness, while this second was indirect witness about their faith. Word about their extraordinary trust in the Lord was carried by word of mouth even further than their verbal witness had gone.[3] "Everywhere" could well mean throughout the whole of the Christian world. Primarily, this is a reference to the conversion of the Thessalonians as a whole, a city that was the Rome of Macedonia, a cosmopolitan metropolis with tentacles that reached everywhere. The evangelistic explosion of the gospel from their church was thus a natural outgrowth of the way their city thought and acted in general. This could be called a campaign greater than that of the Macedonian Alexander the Great, but now the greater conquest was of the eternal gospel rather than the campaigns of a mere conquering king.

Their impact is so great on the rest of the church and evangelistic on the rest of the region that Paul simply says, "Therefore we do not need to say anything about it." In actuality, though, he cannot keep quiet about them, as in 2 Thessalonians 1:4 ("we boast about your perseverance") or 2 Corinthians 8:1–3 ("I testify that they gave as much as they were able"). His point here is that they don't need any more praise, for their fame precedes them everywhere.

*The story of their conversion (1:9–10)*

Paul implied their conversion in verse 8, but now he explicitly discusses it as a major basis of his thankfulness for them. In actuality, though, all of verses 2–10 center on the remarkable story of

---

3. Many see this as restating their evangelistic activity, but it more likely is adding a comment about their reputation going everywhere. This is how I take it here.

their coming to Christ. The first half centers on the report Paul had received in which "they themselves"—that is, the people evangelized by the Thessalonians—reported "what kind of reception you [the Thessalonians] gave us." Paul is referring in part to the reception his mission team received at their initial entrance to Thessalonica. However, the actual term is *eisodon* and means "entrance" rather than "reception," referring more to the manner in which the team entered the city than to the reception the people gave them.

There is an implied contrast between the manner in which they entered and that of prominent orators and politicians who came into the city with all the fanfare and attention-seeking, with trumpets blaring and heralds going forth to proclaim the illustrious personage who has honored the city by coming. It reminds me of our time, with the evening news proclaiming a certain singer or movie star who has come. These are almost sickening days with the attention-getting divas who have made millions by flaunting their looks. Paul, on the other hand, came not pushing himself at all but proclaiming the wondrous gift he was bringing Thessalonica, God's salvation in the gospel.

The first element of the report centered on the mission team and their message. The second element centers on the conversion and response of the Thessalonians themselves. They "turned to God from idols to serve the living and true God." "Turned" (*epistrephō*) was often used for repentance (Hos 14:2; Joel 2:19; Acts 15:19) and is perfect for the idea here. Thessalonica was second only to Athens for the sheer number of idols and temples in their city. From the first of the Ten Commandments on, there is an absolute antithesis between God and idols: "You shall have no other gods before me" (Exod 20:3; Deut 5:7). So Thessalonica was as far from God as it is possible to get. The Greco-Roman people were a superstitious lot, and their gods were important to them. So it took unbelievable courage to "turn from idols," for as in strongly idolatrous cultures today, to reject the family gods is to be rejected by one's family and by society as a whole. To turn to God from idols had quite serious consequences.

However, the key is not what you are turning from but whom you are turning to—"the living and true God." This strengthens the contrast between the eternal living God and the dead idols of the pagan religions as well as the lies behind the myths and the deep truths of the God of Christianity. These two designations are used frequently, especially to contrast him with dead idols and to stress his dynamic power (living—Deut 5:26; 1 Sam 17:36; Isa 65:16; true—2 Chr 15:3; Isa 65:16; Jer 10:10).

As these new believers serve the living and true God, they are experiencing not only his "living" presence in this world but also the vibrant hope (see v. 3) of the heavenly realm (v. 10). Since the living God is also the eternal God, and since we have been adopted as his children, our hope is eternal and centered on the absolute certainty of the second coming of Christ (Titus 2:13; Phil 3:20). Our present is watched over by our vigilant God, and our future is completely secure in the Lord Jesus Christ. As we serve the living God, we at the same time "wait for his Son from heaven" (see also Rom 8:23; 1 Cor 1:7).

This is a key issue for these Christians, as we will see in 4:13–5:10; they were completely uncertain about the timing of Christ's return and whom it would include. Two things they did realize, though, were the fact of his return and that he would come "from heaven." So they knew they had a heavenly inheritance awaiting them, and Paul capitalizes on that.

To stress the intimate relation between Christ and God, Paul chooses to use his sonship; the Father and the Son are acting in concert to make our eternity secure. Moreover, when Christ died he ascended into heaven and God exalted him to "his right hand in the heavenly realms" (Eph 1:20; Ps 110:1; Matt 22:44; Acts 2:33–34; Eph 1:20). So his return "from heaven" will mean the end of the world of evil and the beginning of eternity. In 4:13–5:10 it will constitute both the glorious inheritance of the saints and the destruction of the sinners.

The Greek actually is plural, "from the heavens," and some read this as supporting the idea of several levels of heaven, as in 2 Cor 12:2: "I know a man in Christ who fourteen years ago was caught up to the third heaven." However, the 2 Corinthians passage is probably simply a reflection of Jewish tradition (they at times had three, five, or seven tiers to heaven) rather than an actual description of heaven, and Paul tends to use the singular and the plural "heaven(s)" with no difference of meaning. The NIV "from heaven" captures the meaning well and avoids confusion.

There are three further descriptions of the **parousia** (the return) of the Son. (1) It is defined by God's raising Jesus from the dead, the central proof for the reality of our own future resurrection (1 Cor 15:4, 12–20; see 4:14 below). It is then natural that God would send the resurrected Lord back to raise his people to everlasting life. (2) This resurrected Lord is identified as none other than Jesus, who appeared in Galilee as prophet and Son of God. This Jesus of Nazareth is the very incarnate One who "made himself nothing" and was "found in appearance as a man" (Phil 2:7–8) so he could offer himself as the atoning sacrifice, bear our sins, and bring us salvation. So in union with the God-man, Jesus, we can inherit eternal life when he returns for us.

(3) The name Jesus means "the one who saves" (see Matt 1:21), and so he will rescue "us from the coming wrath." This is an area they were confused, thinking that perhaps those saints who die before Christ returns will fall under God's wrath (4:13–15). Paul is assuring them that this does not describe their future. Some of them were thinking that their intense persecution was the result of the wrath of God. Paul assures them that this is not the case.

Too many in our day center entirely on their future salvation and want to pretend there is no wrath to come. The Bible throughout stresses that there are two interdependent aspects of the Holy

God—his love and his righteous judgment. The wrath of God is part of his holy character and cannot be ignored. Since our world is filled with evil, God must react with wrath to that sinful part of it.

Moreover, by our own actions we cannot solve the sin problem or save ourselves. We are sinful beings and cannot be righteous enough to do so. So God sent his Son to take our sins upon himself, shed his blood to atone for our sins, and thereby "rescue us" from God's wrath. Only this could lead to the promise of 5:9, "God did not appoint us to suffer wrath but to receive salvation through our Lord Jesus Christ." Our future is life, not destruction; joy, not wrath. God will judge, condemn, and destroy this evil world (by fire, 2 Pet 3:10), but the Lord Jesus Christ has saved or rescued us from that future wrath.

———

This opening paragraph shows how much love and concern Paul had for those he had brought to the Lord. His anxiety is obvious, as he knew he had not had sufficient time to teach them and help them grow before he had been forced to leave them. His thanksgiving shows the relief he feels with Timothy's good report about their stance for Christ and perseverance under the pressure of their intense persecution. The report told the team how the faith, love, and hope of these recent converts had led to a vigorous church that persevered under adversity and worked hard on behalf of each other (v. 3).

As Paul reflects on the true situation at Thessalonica, he is overjoyed and thankful for the evidence that God has truly made them his elect and demonstrated his choice by filling their church with his word and power (vv. 4–5). This is all a wonderful model for us, as we too reflect the deep truths of his word and its Spirit-endowed power to undergird us and enable us to be victorious in our daily lives. Moreover, Paul was also thankful that he and his team were given strength by God to exemplify these truths not only in what they said but also in how they lived.

The wondrous results of this story are seen in verses 6–7, as these young Christians provided a model that other churches could emulate. In the midst of a terribly intense persecution they had risen above their circumstances and remained faithful to Christ to such an extent that churches all over the Christian world heard about it and were encouraged to pattern themselves after the Thessalonian example.

Paul tells the story itself in verses 8–10, encapsulating how God can turn desperate situations into triumphant celebration. Their remarkable story became known all over the Christian world, and their faith in Christ was celebrated everywhere. Everyone had worried how these new converts would fare in one of the most idolatrous cities in the empire, especially when they had to face the pressure alone, without Paul to help. However, they soared, and the model they provided inspired people everywhere. Clearly the hope inspired by the truth regarding the return of Christ and the certainty of their future (vv. 9–10) gave them the strength to rise above the pressure of present persecution and to endure the opposition of the pagans surrounding them.

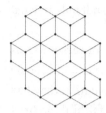

# THE DEFENSE OF PROPER
# CHRISTIAN MINISTRY
(2:1–16)

In this section Paul seems to expand on 1:9, where he contrasted his team's entrance into Thessalonica with the pomp of the itinerant philosophers who sought fame and glory in every town they entered. In the first twelve verses of chapter 2 Paul describes the goals of his mission team when they entered, and in verses 13–16 he tells how they were received by those who later became converts. Paul's tone seems to indicate an apologetic defense of their motives, but he does not identify the group that was criticizing them. This may hint that Paul and his team were being criticized as false philosophers trying to get attention and make a lot of money in Thessalonica.

The problem is deciding who exactly was making the criticisms. Some posit Jewish opponents on the basis of the description of the riot instigated by the synagogue in Acts 17:1–9. Yet in the letter itself, the primary opposition comes from Gentiles. In this sense it would be pagan opposition that Paul is answering. However, since there are no clear indications of actual critics operating here, a growing number of scholars believe the passage isn't apologetic but **paraenetic**, exhorting the readers to follow the example of the mission team in caring and ministering to those around them rather than living for themselves. I believe this latter hypothesis is correct. It is a defense, but defending proper conduct and Christian ministry rather than defending Paul's team against criticism. In a sense, all of verses 1–16 is a model for us to emulate in our own ministries.

## PAUL'S TEAM EXEMPLIFIED PROPER MINISTRY DURING THEIR INITIAL VISIT (2:1-12)

### THE PROPER METHOD FOR MINISTRY (2:1-2)

Building on the thanksgiving section of chapter 1 and especially his discussion of their entry into Thessalonica in verses 5 and 9, Paul centers first on the success of that mission, beginning with causal *gar* ("for," omitted in the NIV), stating that they turned to God because of the mission God sent to them. In other words, God chose his messianic heralds very carefully and sent those to the Thessalonians who could truly make a difference. Paul asks them to remember that original evangelistic event when the team arrived with the gospel. The character he and the others demonstrated is to become a model for their own behavior.

The language of verse 1 is difficult to interpret. Paul says, "our entrance to you was not *ou kenē*." The term means "empty, without result, vain" and could be understood several ways: it could mean (1) that they did not come "empty-handed" but brought something for their benefit; (2) that their visit was not "without results" or a "failure" but had great success; or (3) that the team was not "insincere, without true purpose." The primary issue is whether Paul is discussing the results of their mission or the character of their team. In actuality, we cannot truly separate the two, and Paul probably is thinking of both aspects. Good character produces good results, and the success of their mission was dependent on the Christ-centeredness of their team. Still, in the context of this paragraph, the greater stress is upon their character, so the third translation may be best.

Verse 2 presents the positive side of the point. Their original coming did not lack true purpose; in fact, it proclaimed the gospel in spite of great opposition. He reminds them of the terrible mistreatment he had received in Philippi before coming to Thessalonica the first time (Acts 16:19–40). That shameful treatment consisted of a violent arrest, being stripped in the marketplace and beaten with rods, and then chained to the wall of a filthy prison.

This "strong opposition" continued in Thessalonica (Acts 17:5–9), where Jews jealous of Paul's success started a riot, arrested several of the believers, and forced them to send Paul and Silas away to Berea. The term for "opposition" is *agōn*, an athletic metaphor for the strenuous effort made in an athletic meet, so it could be translated "in spite of agonizing opposition" or "in spite of the antagonism." Far from lacking good motives, they were willing to proclaim the gospel to them in spite of both previous and current hostility from both Jews and Gentiles. They had to overcome insult, shame, and physical abuse, and they did so triumphantly.

The emphasis here is not just on the what (the fact of the successful evangelistic campaign) but even more on the how. They were not victorious on their own or by the power of their personalities. They did so entirely because "with the help of our God we dared to tell you his gospel." The violent actions of the pagans filled them with fear (how could it not), but God's undergirding presence gave them the strength to "dare" to speak. The verb (*parrēsiazomai*) means to have the courage to speak boldly. The intense opposition, far from silencing them, brought out the empowering presence of the Triune Godhead and gave them even greater boldness to proclaim the gospel. Clearly Paul is deflecting attention from himself to God, and that is his message to these beleaguered believers—they too can find the strength in God to rise above all that the world can throw their way. Not only is the mission team sincere and bold as they minister; they are God-centered and Spirit-filled.

## THE PROPER MOTIVE FOR MINISTRY (2:3–4)

Paul now discusses the gospel proclamation itself. Paul's "appeal" is to accept the gospel message, and he wants them to realize that their motives in proclaiming God's salvation were completely devoid of human failure. The word for "appeal," *paraklēsis*, could mean either a word of comfort or a petition. Both connotations are at work here, referring to both the exhortation itself and the appeal to respond to it.

Paul highlights three aspects of the appeal. (1) It "does not spring from error," a phrase meaning it does not contain false information. Some, however, see Paul's words not as intellectual but as moral, meaning without any attempt to deceive, but that is more in the third aspect. Paul was not a false prophet, and his message did not contain false teaching. It could be completely trusted. There were many false teachers in the early church, but Paul and his team were not among them. (2) They were not guilty of having "impure motives" like so many itinerant philosophers in the first century. Some read a sexual connotation into "impure," but that doesn't fit here, and it more likely refers to self-centered, profit-seeking motives. (3) Paul and his team had no intention to "trick" or "deceive" the people; they were not con men whose purpose was only to lure their marks with a false message.

Not only was the message of the gospel filled with truth, but also the messengers were "approved by God" and "entrusted with the gospel" (v. 4). The verb for "approve" is *dokimazō*, referring to a test that is administered in order to approve someone's veracity. Paul and his message have been thoroughly vetted by God himself, and his gospel has the divine seal of approval.

The result of the examination is that God has "entrusted [them] with the gospel." The verb *pisteuō*, which Paul uses here for "entrusted," is the basic New Testament term for "I believe, have faith." Now it is turned around: God has faith in them and trusts them with his truths. If anyone in the world can be believed, it is them. Talk about a final exam! And Paul and his team passed their comps with flying colors. Paul and others have often told their churches to test and examine themselves and their leaders (Rom 14:18; 1 Cor 11:28; 2 Cor 13:5–7; 1 Tim 3:10; 1 John 4:1), and now the ultimate test takes place as God examines Paul and his associates. Shame and judgment await those who fail this test (2 Tim 2:15). I have been part of examining teams where a student who worked on a PhD dissertation for ten years has failed (fortunately, this has not happened often). It is tragic, but failing God's test is worse. Paul and his colleagues, however, passed the test.

Paul is very aware of this test and exclaims, "We are not trying to please people but God, who tests our hearts." Entertainers live only to please people and get them to buy tickets. Too many popular preachers unfortunately fall into the same category. I know of churches that have done sociological studies of the area their church is in so they can tailor their sermons and church programs to the desires and likes of the area. That is the "itching ears" syndrome of 2 Timothy 4:3, shallow teachers who tell people what they want to hear rather than what God wants them to hear. Paul will have none of that. He ministers to please God, not his audience. Integrity in preaching and teaching is proclaiming the message that God puts on your heart, not the one that will increase your popularity.

## DISTANCING THEMSELVES FROM POPULAR SPEAKERS (2:5–8)

### Three disclaimers (2:5–6a)

To further distance themselves from popular street philosophers of the day, Paul utters three denials, paralleling the three negatives of verse 3. Each was a common method used to woo an audience and win their attention. Paul's team, however, sought to win the hearers to God, not to themselves. They wished to bring the people to Christ rather than to talk them into becoming followers of themselves.

(1) "You know we never used flattery": "You know" is actually an independent clause appearing after the demurral, "as you know," showing that Paul is appealing to their personal knowledge of the type of people his team included. The term for flattery, *kolakeia*, is negative and refers to saying nice things about a person in order to take advantage of them, to con them out of money or gain influence over them. The term was used of people of poor moral character and low ethical standards. As in verse 5 Paul is distancing himself from the usual type of visiting speakers who would enter Thessalonica. He was not trying to gain advantage or power over them, for he extolled the Lord, not himself.

(2) "Nor did we put on a mask to cover up greed": As in the first denial, Paul adds an independent statement to emphasize the truth of his words—"God is our witness." Invoking God as witness is frequent in Scripture (Judg 11:10; Job 16:19; Jer 45:2; Rom 1:9; Phil 1:8) to emphasize the truth of a statement. Here it means both the Thessalonians and God himself can now serve as witnesses to their exemplary character. There were no deceptive tactics or hypocrisy in their ministry or message. The image came from Greek plays, where actors would often play several parts and hold masks over their face for each part they played. Paul was not merely pretending or playing a role when he told them of God's salvation. Greed was what drove most itinerant speakers and false teachers. This is very true in our day as well. Cult leaders more often than not know that what they are saying is a lie. They are turning religion into a money-making machine and lining their own pockets by stealing from their followers. Paul for this reason refused to take money but supported himself as a leather worker rather than accepting gifts (2:9 below; see Acts 18:3; 20:34; 1 Cor 4:12).

(3) "We were not looking for praise from people" (v. 6): These are the major two criticisms itinerant philosophers received back then—the desire for money and for praise. Paul makes this more emphatic by adding "not from you or anyone else." As he said in verse 4, "we are not trying to please people but God." He

uses the term *doxa*, "glory," in the sense of "honor" or "fame." We must remember that in the first-century such traveling speakers were the primary entertainment, the movie stars of their day. So nearly all of them put themselves on display and did anything they could to become famous, the Ciceros of their time. Sounds like a few people in our day too, doesn't it? It is amazing to think of the number who have made millions simply by flaunting their curves or their six-packs. Paul wants to make certain he is not linked with that crowd.

### Choosing the path of humility (2:6b–7a)

Paul and his team could have come demanding fame and fortune. "As apostles of Christ we could have asserted our authority."[1] They refused to demand glory from the Thessalonians, though as apostles they could have done so. There are two issues. Why the plural "apostles"? It seems Paul is including Silas and Timothy as apostles as well as himself. Yet he has never done so elsewhere in his epistles. Some think he includes Silas[2] but not Timothy, but that is supposition with no proof. It is probably better to see Paul elevating his associates and connecting them with his office. He did so in 1:1, making them coauthors of the letter, and he could be doing so here as well, placing them under his umbrella as an apostle. The term itself (*apostolos*) contains the idea of an Aramaic *shaliach*, one sent with the authority of the sender (in this case God and Paul). So they acted in concert with Paul under the sending power of God himself.

The second issue is the phrase behind "asserted our authority," *en barei*, which literally means "to be a burden" and could refer

---

1. The Greek text has this as part of v. 7, while the NIV, in order to stress the connection with v. 6a, makes it the last part of v. 6. I prefer the Greek order, but for the sake of clarity, we will follow the NIV order.

2. Silas could have been a witness of the resurrection, the criterion for the apostolic office (Acts 1:22; 1 Cor 9:1, 15:8).

to Paul demanding that they support his team financially (as in 2 Cor 11:9). Paul would then be making a fourth denial, that they had refused to be an economic burden on them. But this Greek term is hardly ever used this way, and most scholars prefer a figurative thrust, to "assert authority" or demand to be treated as important. This fits the idea of glory and praise in verse 6a and would constitute an even stronger denial: they as apostles could have demanded honor and glory from the Thessalonians but refused to do so.

Instead of seeking fame, they did the opposite in their ministry. They "were like young children among you." Here there is an issue with how the manuscripts read. The better Greek manuscripts (a third-century papyrus, codices Sinaiticus, Vaticanus, Ephraemi, Bezae, and others) have the term *nēpioi* ("infant"), but a few (Alexandrinus, secondary copies of the codices above) have the closely related *ēpioi* ("gentle"), and that fits the following metaphor of a nursing mother much better. It seems jarring to proceed from the image of infants to the image of a nursing mother in successive clauses. So most translations have opted for "gentle" (KJV, NKJV, NRSV, ESV, NASB, CSB), with a few opting for "infants" (NIV, NLT, NET, LEB). However, the stronger evidence favors "infant," and the common rule in text criticism is that the clumsier or "less likely" version is to be preferred. (This is because early church copyists tended to smooth out readings rather than make them more difficult.) So all in all, the reading "young children" or "infants" is the preferred reading here.

Paul is saying that rather than demand that their importance be recognized and they be elevated to the highest status that they deserve, they willingly take the lowest spot and have become "infants" or those of lowest status among them. This is similar to Philippians 2:6–7, where Paul says that Jesus, who is God of very God in reality, relinquished this status in his incarnation and became our slave. Paul relinquished his status as apostle and became a virtual infant in order to serve them. He is obviously not thinking of the helpless state of small children in his metaphor here but of their lower status. The metaphor of serving the church comes next in verse 7b.

### Choosing the path of caring and sharing (2:7b–8)

As Jesus became a slave who served humanity (Phil 2:6–7), Paul and his cohorts became a "nursing mother" who cared for the Thessalonians. Rather than the usual term, he chooses *trophos*, a nursing mother who suckles infants. This is not a wet nurse. The emphasis is on her love that leads her to care and share everything with her children. Note these are "her children" (*ta heautēs tekna*), stressing the family metaphor. The term for "cares" is *thalpō*, a strong word for deep-seated caring, as some put it, "cherishing" her children.

In verse 8 Paul deepens the imagery, showing that the deep-seated, tender caring was due to the intense love they felt for these new believers. The NIV changes the order of clauses in the verse. In actuality this is framed with statements of deep affection. Two causal statements frame the sentence, saying literally: "because we longed and cared for you so much, we were delighted to commit ourselves to share with you ... because you have become beloved to us." The intense family language deepens the sense of Paul and his team's love and caring for them. The mission team is both mother (v. 8) and father (v. 11), and they are so filled with love that they focus entirely on caring and sharing with their new family members, basically their children in the Lord.

The picture is that of an intense longing that leads to love and a desire to share everything with the other. The verb *eudokeō* can mean to "delight in" something or to "resolve" or "determine" to do something. Both the will and the emotions are involved. Here both aspects are likely included. Their great affection gave them joy in deciding to serve these people with everything they have. They committed themselves to sharing not just the gospel but themselves as well. The itinerant speakers would take and share little with the towns they invaded (term chosen deliberately). Paul's team took nothing but gave of themselves totally to serve these people whom they loved so deeply. They not only refused to lord over their new followers; they determined to give of themselves totally, to fill the Thessalonians with all the loving care they could and share the depths of their souls with them.

## THE PAST CARE THE TEAM BESTOWED ON THEM (2:9–12)

### Their intense labor (2:9)

As in verse 1 Paul asks them to "remember" the past actions of the team in order to prove the depth of their loving care. Their self-sacrificial attitude (v. 8) and their refusal to allow greed to dictate their actions (v. 5) was demonstrated in the "toil and hardship" that described their early ministry. The two terms connote not just hard work but also the fatigue and pain associated with it. Instead of demanding money and support from them, they "worked night and day in order not to be a burden to anyone." We know that the Philippian church sent money to help them (Phil 4:15–16), but they had to work as well. Probably Paul engaged in the same type of tentmaking as at Corinth in Acts 18:3 and Ephesus in Acts 22:34–35. This almost certainly means he was a leather worker, not just making and repairing tents but making other kinds of leather goods as well.

The ministry demands in addition to the manual labor meant they had to "work night and day"—a common idiom in Greek—to support themselves. The purpose of this hard work was so that they would not "be a burden to anyone while we preached the gospel of God to you." Elsewhere he declared his right to receive financial aid in ministry (1 Cor 9:3–6, 9–12a), but both then and here in Thessalonica he did not demand that right so that he would not hinder the gospel (1 Cor 9:12b) or be a financial burden on the people (here).

The gospel proclamation probably took place at the work-place. There is evidence that this was permitted behavior by philosophers, and Paul, Silas, and Timothy likely proclaimed the gospel and engaged in discussions with people while working with leather. Still, the demands of the two meant they possibly had to begin before dawn and work past sunset, the normal hours for manual labor. They would usually take a lengthy late afternoon break, but Acts 19:9–10 shows that Paul would even take that time to proclaim the gospel, preaching and dialoguing in the lecture hall of Tyrannus during the afternoon hours at Ephesus. The main point of this verse is to show that Paul and the others were willing to work themselves to the bone rather than hinder the gospel by demanding support from the Thessalonians.

*Their fatherly care for the Thessalonians (2:10–12)*

In verses 10–12 Paul continues to emphasize that they "remember" (v. 9) that which they witnessed about the apostolic team, not only their hard work (v. 9) but also their exemplary character in the way they conducted themselves. Paul also frames these verses with the presence and reality of God. God is also a witness[3] of Paul's high character in verse 10, and the section ends by reminding the readers that it is God who has called them to his kingdom (v. 12b). They witnessed to what was visible; God witnessed to what was not. Interestingly too, this moves from the original time when the Thessalonians had been evangelized to the time after the church was established, probably the short period when they were pastoring and teaching the new converts before Paul was forced to leave.

During that period, the believers discovered "how holy, righteous and blameless we were among you who believed." The emphasis is on their righteous conduct as well as their character. As the new believers observed how the team acted spiritually before God and ethically in their relations with them, they could see their true character in the way they conducted themselves. It

---

3. Paul invokes Deut 19:15, the demand for two or three witnesses, to stress the truthfulness of what he is saying here.

is generally thought that "holy" (the adverb *hosiōs* highlights how they exemplified this) stresses the God side and "righteous" the human side of their conduct. They lived "set apart" lives that centered on God and were both "righteous" and "just" (both aspects of *dikaios* are part of the meaning here) in the way they related to those around them. In sum, their "blameless" behavior was evident to all. They could find no fault with the team in the eyes of God or the eyes of people. These three flawless men were models of behavior to all who observed them. If there was any question of whom to believe, these holy and righteous men or the charlatans who addressed them as so-called philosophers or political voices, there was no contest.

In verse 11 Paul again asks them to recall what they "know" about him and his team, and again it is the manner (Greek *hōs*, "how," translated "that" in the NIV) of their dealings with the Thessalonians. In verse 7 Paul said they acted as a mother caring for her children, and now they conduct themselves like a father lovingly overseeing the lives of his children and instructing them in the Christian life. There is no verb in the Greek, so one must be supplied on the basis of the context. Since the metaphor is a father raising his children, versions supply ones like "deals with" (NIV, NRSV) or "treated" (NLT, NET, LEB). There is strong emphasis on "each one of you," and Paul is appealing to every one of the believers there to recall the righteous, blameless behavior of the mission team as they helped the church to grow spiritually.

There are two different developments in the father metaphor: (1) In verse 7 they were "infants" and took the lowest status among them, serving them; in verse 7b they are a nursing mother, caring for them; and here they are fathers, raising and training them in the Lord. (2) Paul is now doubly a father to them, bringing them into this world through the new birth and now bringing them up and training them in the new life they have entered. Paul intends both aspects, reminding the Thessalonians of how deeply the mission team became part of the family in Thessalonica. As a mother, he loves them and cares for them, helping them grow. As a father, he nurtures and trains them, helping them mature.

All ancient societies were patriarchal, and the father was the ruler of the family. In the Jewish family, the mother had control of the children until age five and of the daughters after that, training them in matters of the household. The fathers took the sons after age five, training them in Torah and increasingly in their own careers as carpenters, tentmakers, and so on. There was a great deal of emphasis on the affection between a father and his children, as well as on the moral instruction that must take place. Parents were to be obeyed implicitly by the children and honored throughout their lives. Paul here is drawing out the loving training of the children by the spiritual "fathers" in the faith.

As I said at the beginning of this section, Paul intends this as a model for the church. We in modern churches would do well to realize how much emphasis the early church gave to proper instruction of the members of the church and to the deep love and care that lay behind it. One of the great needs of our day is for quality Bible studies and discipleship training in our churches.

In verse 12 Paul provides a second set of descriptions of the level of care Paul and his associates gave their followers. In verse 10 Paul named three spiritual qualities of the team itself; now he provides three depictions of the kind of care they bestowed on the Thessalonians. They were "encouraging, comforting and urging [them] to live lives worthy of God." The first verb, *parakaleō*, is language of exhortation and comfort, and while the NIV's "encouraging" is viable, the Greek more likely describes the exhortation of moral instruction based on the gospel and biblical truth. This is a major verb for the teaching ministry of the early church. The second verb, *paramytheomai*, does speak of consoling or comforting others and is often used to encourage people to certain actions. The third verb, *martyromai*, is best known for bearing witness but also means to urge or implore a person to proper conduct.

The three verbs in the context most likely are somewhat synonymous. Several commentators along with the NIV see nuances of comfort and consolation in light of the persecution they were undergoing, but I do not see that in this context. All the terms center on nuances of ethical exhortation and probably connote ideas of encouraging these new Christians to yield to Christ and the Spirit in their walk through life.

The purpose of this exhortation and urging is to encourage them "to live lives worthy of God." Paul here is a loving father appealing to and commanding his children to exemplify the kind of conduct that pleases God. The verb behind "live lives" is *parapateō*, describing the Christian "walk." Here it is to "walk worthily of God," a phrase that parallels Colossians 1:10 ("walk worthily of the Lord") and Ephesians 4:1 (walk "worthily of your calling"). The idea of the Christian walk is a favorite image of Paul's to describe living a life and conducting one's self as God wishes. To be "worthy of God" is to live according to his standards, to please him in all that you do.

This God whose standards you follow is the God "who calls you into his kingdom and glory." The saints are "called," which, as in 1:4, makes them God's "elect." The present-tense "calls" stresses the ongoing nature of God's election. This is the underlying reason God's people can live lives that are "worthy of God," for he has chosen and empowered them. The emphasis is not on their past conversion but their present life in the Lord. God continues to call them to himself and give them strength to live victoriously in him. It entails a call to a life of holiness (2:10; 4:7), sanctification (4:3), and a desire to please God (4:1).

"His kingdom and glory" are interconnected. It is quite possible that "kingdom" refers to the present realm and "glory" the future and final realm that will be ours.[4] In this sense there is an already/

---

4. The majority of commentators believe that the two are synonymous, but I think Paul is addressing the present and future kingdoms in his choice of these two terms.

not yet reality behind what Paul is saying. At Christ's first coming he inaugurated the kingdom of God in this world, and a salvation-historical shift took place. We now live in the already. God's kingdom has entered this world, and we are a part of it. We await the not-yet, the arrival of the final "glory" at Christ's second coming. The kingdom is not a place but the reign of God over his world, and it has already begun. Paul will soon be correcting their misunderstandings about the final "glory" that will be theirs (4:13–5:10). The present troubles and animosity they are experiencing will give way to a glorious and joyous eternity.

## THE THESSALONIANS RECEIVE THE WORD AND IMITATE THE JUDEAN CHRISTIANS (2:13–16)

This becomes a second thanksgiving after 1:2, as Paul expresses his thanks for the wonderful reception his team found among the Thessalonians when they brought the gospel to them. In the previous twelve verses we learned of the mission and the exemplary character of the mission team, and now we learn of the original response of the converts to their ministry among them. As I noted in the introduction to 2:1–12, the purpose is paraenetic: Paul wants us to follow the example and imitate the Thessalonians in exactly the way they emulated the models first of Paul (1:6) and then of the Judean churches (2:14). We need to follow both reactions: (1) When we hear the word of God proclaimed in sermons and lessons, we must recognize it as the word of God and be first attentive to it and then obedient to it. (2) When we pass through hard times, we need to be like the Judeans and the Thessalonians in our dependence on the Lord and his strength so as to endure and triumph over our trials.

### ACCEPTING THE WORDS AS THE WORD OF GOD (2:13)

Paul has been thankful for these incredible churches throughout the letter, and some even go so far as to think the thanksgiving section extends through this material to 3:13. That is overstating the case, but it is true that everywhere we look in these opening two chapters, he is thankful for their wondrous response to the gospel and to Paul's team. An interesting study would be to contrast the Thessalonians with the Corinthians—total acceptance versus total opposition to his teaching. The Greek text begins with "and because of this," and scholars debate whether this looks back to the ministry of Paul's team (2:1-12) or ahead to their reception of the gospel (2:13). Opinion is evenly divided, but in the context it seems more likely that it looks ahead. The emphasis is on Paul's "continual" thankfulness for that response, showing that the Thessalonian response was ongoing and deep. Every time Paul thought of them he did so thanking God for them.

There is a play on words with "word of God" here. The first refers to the missionary proclamation of the team, "when you received the word of God, which you heard from us." The proclamation of the gospel is called "the word of God" because it originated from God, and the leading of the Spirit lay behind it. This does not mean their sermons were Scripture in themselves, but they faithfully contained God's word and flowed out of it.

Two related verbs describe their reception of it, "received" and "accepted." This is language of the passing on of tradition in Judaism and the early church, similar to 1 Corinthians 15:3, the earliest creed on the death and resurrection of Christ: "For what I received I passed on to you." Paul also uses this kind of language to refer to the reception of the gospel in Galatians 1:11-12. They received it not just from the preaching of the apostles but more importantly from God himself, and they "accepted" it as such.

There are two implications of this for us today. First of all, proper sermons stem not just from the preacher but from the God who led the preacher to proclaim his word to the congregation. Second, the preacher is under intense responsibility to make certain it is God's message that he is proclaiming. The depth of the preaching and teaching that goes on in churches matters greatly. Paul says it well to Timothy in 2 Timothy 2:15: "Do your best to present yourself to God as one approved, a worker who does not need to be ashamed and who correctly handles the word of truth." All too many teachers will stand before God ashamed due to the shallowness of their messages. One of the major prayers I have for this series is that these commentaries may help render shallow preaching unnecessary.

Their acceptance was extensive, recognizing it "not as a human word, but as it actually is, the word of God." My constant prayer is also that this can be said of my teaching and preaching, that my messages will never be spoken off the top of my head, so to speak, but will always be uttered out of deep study and ongoing prayer. In other words, God made certain the message they proclaimed was his inspired message, and the Thessalonians recognized and accepted it for what it was, the word of God.

The proof of its divine origin was seen in their lives, in the fact that it "is indeed at work in you who believe." The evidence of its reality was provided in the quality of their daily lives. The fruit of the Spirit was evident in them (Gal 5:22–23), and they lived as "more than conquerors" (Rom 8:37) in the midst of terrible times of persecution. Oh, that we could say the same! The verb "is at work" (*energeitai*) speaks of the continual work/energy of God that is active in them and giving them the energy to rise above their difficulties. Out of God's work in us comes the power to triumph over all the crises of life.

### Imitating the Suffering Churches of Judea (2:14)

Paul saw the positive reaction of the Thessalonians in their response both to the word and to the persecution that followed. Instead of bemoaning their fate and complaining that God had failed them, they accepted their bad lot as a natural part of following Christ and "became imitators of God's churches in Judea, which are in Christ." In their willingness to endure, they showed the depth of their reception of the word. "Judea" does not mean only the official territory but includes the churches of the whole of Palestine, including Galilee. So we now have a third group they are imitating, the Judean churches as well as Paul's team and the Lord in 1:6. Imitation is part of discipleship. The disciples try to emulate their spiritual mentors as the mentors seek to emulate Christ. These churches are "in Christ Jesus," meaning they are not only Christian but that they draw their strength and identity from Christ.

It is completely logical that the people who crucified Christ would also persecute his followers. The persecution of the disciples in Acts is well chronicled there, from their arrest, imprisonment, and beating of the disciples in 4:13-21 and 5:13-40, to the stoning of Stephen and scattering of the believers in 7:54-8:3, to the martyrdom of James and imprisonment of Peter in 12:1-19, and finally to the arrest and attempts to kill Paul in chapters 21-23. The Jewish opposition could hardly have been more intense. Paul was one of the leaders of this antagonism until his conversion (Acts 8:58-9:2, 26:10-11; Gal 1:23; Phil 3:6).

The intensity of the persecution in Thessalonica is seen in Paul's comparison: "You suffered from your own people the same things those churches suffered from the Jews." So this was not occasional suffering but ongoing and intense affliction. The beginnings are described in Acts 17:4-9. Paul's success in his synagogue ministry provoked many Jews to jealousy (they did not have the success among the Gentiles Paul did), and they rounded up some troublemakers from the seedy part of town and started a riot. The persecution here is a Gentile movement, with *symphyletai* meaning "fellow countrymen." This is in keeping with 1:9, which indicates the great majority of the converts were Gentiles who had "turned from idols." This doesn't mean there were no Jewish Christians there, only that there were few.

In Judea the suffering came "from the Jews." Some think this should be restricted to the geographical territory of Judea, thus not including the churches of Samaria and Galilee, on the grounds that *Ioudaioi* ("Jews") has a technical sense of the people in the territory of Judea. Others extend this reference beyond the borders of Palestine to Jewish persecution in general, but in verse 15 Paul will show he has in mind the homeland of Judea and Galilee here.

## IDENTIFYING THE PERSECUTORS (2:15–16)

The rest of this passage centers on three facts about the persecutors—what they have done (v. 15a), what kind of people they are (vv. 15b–16a), and the divine judgment they are bringing upon themselves (v. 16b). It is very interesting that while this paragraph begins with persecution "from your own people," the rest of the section centers only on Jewish hostility, from their vicious actions in verse 15a to their evil character in verse 15b and then to the consequences—God's wrath against them in verse 16b. Here he stipulates three things the Jews have done to show that their current animosity has been around a long time.

### Their evil actions (2:15a)

The first evil action is the central one: they "killed the Lord Jesus." Certainly only a handful were there that fateful day, and probably the majority would not have wanted this to happen. However, virtually the whole nation ended up rejecting Jesus as God's Messiah and in this way was complicit in his death. When Pilate washed his hands and the bystanders said, "His blood is on us and on our children" (Matt 27:24–25), Jewish guilt was established. They had not just murdered the man Jesus but the Lord of all. It is the exalted Lord whom they put on the cross, and he will return as Judge of all. Many have demurred against the strongly negative tone of this indictment of the Jews, but we must remember that Paul's purpose is to show that the Gentiles are equally guilty in their own rejection and persecution of God's people. Jewish guilt is not the main point; the guilt of all who turn against Jesus and his people is the point. Still, they stand under the wrath of God in their guilt.

Second, these are the same people who had killed the prophets. This is a common emphasis in both the Old Testament (1 Kgs 18:4;

19:10; 2 Chr 24:21; Neh 9:26) and the New Testament (Acts 7:52; Rom 11:3; Heb 11:32-37) to show the extent of the rebellion of God's apostate people. Note the emphasis here—those the Jews killed were those sent by God with authority over them. Theirs was not only rebellion against God; it entailed also self-worship and usurping authority for themselves.

Third, they "drove us out," both originally from the homeland Israel in the scattering of the followers of Jesus in Acts 8:1-3 and in the forced exodus of Paul and Silas from Thessalonica in Acts 17:10 in the original persecution there, as had happened to Paul often (Acts 13:50; 14:6, 20; 16:39-40; 17:14; 20:1). The opposition to Paul and his team echoed the hatred of Jesus, and now was echoed in what the Thessalonians were going through.

### The kind of people they are (2:15b-16a)

As he often does, Paul looks first to the vertical relationship to God ("displease God") and then to the horizontal relationship to those around ("hostile to everyone"). In some sense the idea of displeasing God seems a little weak after the terrible claims about their murderous rampages and pogroms against the saints. However, it is a major feature of Paul's spiritual and ethical teaching, describing the final goal of living the Christian life (Rom 12:1-2; 1 Cor 7:32; 2 Cor 5:9; Gal 1:10; Col 1:10; 2 Tim 2:4). To fail to please God is to bring divine judgment on your head, as we will see in verse 16b. The concept sums up the ultimate goal of both testaments. In 4:1 below the primary desire of the Thessalonians must be to please God, and Paul extols them to "do this more and more." He links it with the process of sanctification and purity (4:3). So pleasing God is everything.

In their earthly relationships they are "hostile to everyone." Even though we would expect this to turn to the Gentile persecutors in Thessalonica, as in 3:4-5 and 2 Thessalonians 1:4-12, it is Jewish hostility here. In Acts 17:1-5 it was the Jews who instigated Gentile opposition, and so Paul is beginning with the roots of the antagonism against the new believers there. Jewish contempt against Gentiles was well known in the ancient world and often written about by Gentile writers. Tacitus, a Roman historian, talked of their "hostility and hatred toward all people" (*Histories* 5.2.2). Paul is saying that this universal hostility is a reflection of the insular attitude of the Jewish people throughout their history. Gentile conversion to them had one major purpose—to prove the superiority of Judaism. The Jewish people never followed the attitude of their God toward the Gentiles. They ignored the Abrahamic covenant promise that "all peoples on earth will be blessed through you" (Gen 12:3).

In verse 16a Paul narrates the actions that grew out of this hostility. They sought to "keep us from speaking to the Gentiles so that they may be saved." This means opposition to the Gentile mission of Paul's team and refers to both the Jewish hostility seen in Acts 17:5–9. The verb (*kōlyō*) means to "hinder" or "prevent" and describes efforts to waylay the team's missionary efforts. They did not want them to succeed in any way. They did not stop with opposition to the team's efforts to win their fellow Jews; they did not want them to succeed with the Gentiles either.

The present tense of the verb shows it goes beyond the specific instance at Thessalonica. Their universal hostility results in continuous persecution of God's people and opposition to any and all missionary efforts. They did not want these upstart Christian preachers to "save" anyone. There is no proclamation of the gospel without the offering of God's salvation to the hearers. This is what the enemies of the church wanted to stop. They wanted to eradicate Christianity completely.

### The divine judgment they are facing (2:16b)

"In this way" translates the Greek *eis to*, meaning "with the result that." Paul is showing what the displeasing actions and massive hostility are actually leading to. He presents it in terms of cause and effect. As a result of the evil actions and attitudes of the persecutors, "they always heap up their sins to the limit," which then leads to divine judgment. From the story of the tower of Babel, when humans tried to reach up to heaven with their human achievements, a frequent image in Scripture has been people "piling up" or "heaping up" their sins. In Genesis 15:16 the Amorites were allowed by God to inhabit the land because their sin had "not yet reached its full measure," and in Daniel 8:23 it is when the rebels "have become completely wicked" that the end times will come. Jesus used this image in Matthew 23:31–32 when he told the scribes and Pharisees who admitted they had "murdered the prophets" to "complete what your ancestors started," literally "fill up the measure of your ancestors."

On the other side of the coin, this image is applied to those suffering persecution in what is called the "messianic woes," stating that God has established a certain amount of suffering to be endured by the Messiah and his community, and when that amount is filled up, the end will come (Col 1:24; Rev 6:11). Paul's point is that these evil opponents have used up all the mercy God has extended them because they have piled up their sins to the limit, so God's judgment is soon to arrive. The Jewish people have used up the mercy of God. Their long history of repeated falls from grace is now at an end. The cycles of sin, apostasy, judgment, temporary repentance, and forgiveness cannot be restricted to the period of the judges. The entire history of the nation from Abraham to the time of Paul was characterized by this sad cycle, but the time is up and judgment is here.

So "the wrath of God has come upon them at last." The difficulty is to determine the question of time. Is the judgment present or future? It cannot be the final judgment sometime in the future, for the aorist-tense Greek word *ephthasen* means "has arrived" and somehow must connote that "God's judgment is here." So those scholars who have understood it as a proleptic anticipation of the imminent end must be wrong.

The meaning of the concluding *eis telon* is debated. It can be translated "at last" with NIV, NRSV, NLT, ESV, but it could also mean "completely, to the uttermost" (KJV, NKJV, NASB, NET), "to the end" (LEB), "finally" (NJB), or "forever" (several scholars). In the context, with the great amount of teaching in these two letters on the final day of judgment (1 Thess 5:1–10; 2 Thess 1:7–10, 2:8–12), we must separate this from those passages. This must denote a tragic event soon to arrive (the already rather than the not-yet) that will demonstrate God's wrath against these rebellious Jews. Scholars have suggested several events, such as their forced expulsion from Rome by edict of the emperor Claudius in AD 49 or the thousands of Jews slaughtered by the Romans in that same year in Jerusalem (both near the time of the writing of this letter). Also possible is the terrible famine of AD 47 or the destruction of Jerusalem in AD 68–70. Any or all of these would suffice to prove Paul's point— Jewish obduracy brings God's wrath down upon them, both now and in the future.

———

The key to this passage is to understand that Paul intended it to be ethical exhortation. The Thessalonian readers *and we ourselves* are to read it as a model and apply it to ourselves. So we should apply this description of the original missionary campaign in Thessalonica to our own church strategy. First, we must make sure our ministry methods and motives are God-centered and Spirit-led. We first must be deeply trying to glorify the Lord and not ourselves. Second, we must refuse to be shallow and just touch the surface in our teaching but must proclaim the word and the gospel deeply and challenge our people to live for him, not themselves (vv. 1–4).

A critical point for us today is the need to avoid the techniques of popular speakers (and preachers) who seek to entertain rather than challenge the people (vv. 5–8). The central stress is on the absence of greed and self-serving and the undergirding foundation of the ministry in love, care, and service. I rejoice deeply when

I meet a well-known Christian leader who is filled with humility, and it happens often. I believe most of them sincerely love their congregations and want to serve them. Still, I often think of a person I met a while ago who had served in several megachurches and said that in his opinion, most of these famous pastors were narcissists. Fortunately that hasn't been my experience, but I know it is all too frequently the case. There is no excuse for pride, not when we follow Christ and have the Spirit. We ought to be loving, caring, humble proclaimers of God's truths.

The next section (vv. 9–12) models the loving care that should characterize all ministry. Paul and his team were nursing mothers and loving fathers to their children in the faith, and that was evident in everything they did. Paul pictures a father encouraging his children to lead lives that please their Father in heaven. As the people to whom we minister watch our lives, they must see how set apart we are for God and how rightly we relate to them. They must see the love that lies behind all our dealings with them.

The rest of this section (vv. 13–16) turns to the reception of the mission by the Thessalonian converts, and here we turn our attention from the ministers to the people in our churches. The prime characteristic builds on what we have just said: the ministers proclaim the word of God; the people accept the messages as centered on God's word and respond with changed lives. When we face the kind of suffering these original responders did, whether persecution like they had or trials in general, we follow their lead and imitate the triumphant saints of the past. They rose above their suffering and found victory, and we can too (see Jas 1:2–4 and 1 Pet 1:6–7 on this).

Finally, Paul describes the Jewish opposition as it relates to the church and to God. As for the church, the Jews wanted to remove them from this earth. They opposed both Jewish and Gentile evangelization and sought to cause it to fail completely. Their persecution was as intense as it possibly could be. However, it would fail, and as a result they faced the wrath of God in the present as well as the future. The emphasis is on the guaranteed protection and final victory of God's mission in and through the church.

Most of us will not go through anything as severe as these people did, but we in our lesser trials still need to remind ourselves of the truths stated here: that God will vindicate us and reward us for our sacrifices, and that "in all things God works for our good" (Rom 8:28). Like the Thessalonians, we can entrust ourselves to him in hard times.

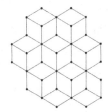

# PAUL'S DESIRE TO SEE THE THESSALONIANS AGAIN
## (2:17–3:13)

I n 2:1–12 Paul discussed the beginnings of his relationship with the Thessalonian church—the apostolic mission of evangelism that brought them to Christ. In verses 14–16 he recalled the Jewish opposition and persecution that brought great suffering. Now he turns to the event that separated them from each other—the Jewish and Gentile persecution that forced Paul and Silas to flee to Berea (Acts 17:10). Now in this section he discusses his forced absence from them—a separation he deeply regrets but cannot reverse because of that continued persecution brought about by Satanic activity. So there are two major trials burdening him—his absence from them and the severe persecution they are undergoing. Several believe that he is also concerned by the fact that outside opponents might use his absence to impugn the quality of his concern for them. There is not a lot of evidence for this, but it must remain a possibility.

So there are four parts and emphases in this section—his intense longing to see them (2:17–20), the fact-finding mission of Timothy (3:1–5), Timothy's excellent report in spite of the severe persecution (3:6–10), and Paul's renewed hopes for them (3:11–13).

## PAUL LONGS TO BE WITH THEM (2:17–20)

The very tone of his comments here will prove to the Thessalonians how deeply he cares. His dialogue is laced with affectionate concern. His forced departure came much too early, and as we will see in chapters 4 and 5 he had not had sufficient time to deepen their theological awareness and prepare them for the hard times that were coming. He wishes he could be with them and is so concerned he cannot even continue his mission until he knows how it has gone with them. So he is waiting in Athens and then in Corinth for Timothy's report.

### Efforts to See Them (2:17)

The focus radically changes as well. Verses 13–16 were all about "they," the Jews and their enmity toward all things Christian. Now it is "but … we," signaling that Paul is returning the focus to himself and his team. This entails a radical change from language of indictment and divine wrath to language of loving care. Paul has moved from his enemies to his "brothers and sisters." He is their father in 1:11, giving critical advice, and now he is their "brother," longing to be with them.

The depth of Paul's longing is seen in the metaphor he chooses: "when we were orphaned by being separated from you." This is actually a fifth switch in the family language of this section—from infants (2:7) to nursing mother (2:8) to father (2:11) to brother/sister (2:17a) to orphan (2:17b). He loves and cares so thoroughly for these disciples of his that he sees himself as every kind of family member with respect to them. He chooses the orphan image[1] to express not just the separation but also the deep pain that goes with it. So he depicts himself bereft of love and companionship and wandering the streets (often the fate of orphans) in his despair.

---

1. In the ancient world, an "orphan" could be a child separated from parents or a parent separated from children. The particular verb used here (*aporphanizō*) is always used of orphaned children, so that is likely the metaphor here.

He has come full circle with respect to them, but his affection for them has continued through it all.

Two qualifications mitigate the circumstances. First, it occurred just a "short time" ago. Very little time has passed, but it seems much longer to Paul, because he longs to be with them so badly. So the pain is even sharper since it took place quite recently. Second, he wants them to understand that to him the separation is "in person, not in thought." He may be physically absent from them, but his heart and mind are still with them. The sooner he can be with them, the better.

The reality of the hurt they felt at the separation is seen in their reaction to it: "out of our intense longing we made every effort to see you." Paul chooses the strongest language he can, with two superlatives—the deepest longing and the greatest effort. They did everything they could to get back to these friends and disciples, even postponing their mission itinerary until they knew how things were going. Paul wants them to know that none of them wanted to be apart from the Thessalonians, and in fact they were doing everything they could to get back to them.

## SATAN'S OBSTACLES (2:18)

The original intention of Paul and Silas had been to return to Thessalonica as soon as the heat died down, but apparently it never did. He repeats in different language what he said in verse 17: "We wanted to come to you—certainly I, Paul, did, again and again." He wants them to know it was quite personal with him. The stress on the great efforts made to return continues, and the intensity of his emotions led him to do so time and time again. We don't know when these attempts took place, but most likely he kept trying while he was waiting in Athens (Acts 17:16-34).

Every time they tried to return, they were hindered—"Satan blocked our way." Their attempts to return were so great, and obstacles set up against them so severe that they could only explain them by recognizing the Satanic activity behind them. The verb *enkoptō* is a military metaphor for "blocking" a road by cutting holes and slits in it to hinder carts and horses from traveling on them. So Paul is using spiritual-warfare language to highlight the serious obstacles set up against them. We are not told what specific roadblocks were erected against them, only that Satan was behind them. Scholars have suggested three possibilities: the persecution that was raging there; the bond that Jason and the local Christians had to put up with the city officials (Acts 17:9); or an illness like the "thorn in the flesh" of 2 Corinthians 12:7 that put him on his back. Any of these as well as something we cannot know are possible.

The main thing we know is that Satan wanted to see the mission in Thessalonica fail and so provided opposition at every turn. This reflects the later statement in Ephesians 6:12 that "our struggle is not against flesh and blood, but against the rulers, against the authorities, against the powers of this dark world and against the spiritual forces of evil in the heavenly realms." His strategy is to find an area of weakness and tempt the believer (1 Cor 7:5; 1 Thess 3:5), defeating them spiritually and hindering the work of God in them (2 Cor 2:11; 1 Pet 5:8).

## PAUL'S GLORY AND JOY (2:19–20)

Paul now spells out his true feelings about them. He had no neutrality whatsoever in his heart response to them, and this certainly explains why he kept trying to get back to the Thessalonians. This is definitely a spiritual parent telling his children how he feels about them. He starts with a rhetorical question: "For what is our hope, our joy, or the crown in which we will glory in the presence of our Lord Jesus when he comes?" Paul likes to say things in threes (see 1:3; 2:3, 5), and that is the case here as well.

"Hope," of course, is centered on the Triune Godhead, for instance in 1:3, where Paul lauds their "endurance inspired by hope in our Lord Jesus Christ." In 1 Peter 1:3 Peter says the new birth leads to "a living hope through the resurrection of Jesus Christ." In the early church hope was "living" in the sense that it is dynamic, concrete, and based on the certainty of the final resurrection in which we will all participate at the **parousia** (the "coming" of Christ). Here this theme takes an unusual turn when he designates the Thessalonians themselves as "our hope." Yet this is a theme in Paul. He tells the Philippians he will "boast" of them as his reward in heaven (Phil 2:16) and calls them "my joy and crown" (Phil 4:1; also here in v. 19); he calls the Corinthians "the seal of my apostleship" (1 Cor 9:2). He considers churches who are faithful to the Lord to be his **eschatological** reward. The reward of Paul in heaven is intimately interdependent with the churches he has established, a perspective every Christian leader today should emulate.

This continues in the other two here: "our joy ... the crown in which we will glory." They are his "joy" not just in the sense that he is overjoyed with the way they have turned out spiritually. This is deeper than that. They are his joy in the Lord, as in 3:9: "all the joy we have in the presence of our God because of you." This is an eschatological joy, as their walk with Christ will result in their own victorious crown at his return, which Paul will share in. Our rewards in heaven will not just be for the fruit of the Spirit; our rewards will be people in whom we have invested ourselves and who have grown under our influence.

Not only are they his "joy"; they are his "crown in which we will glory [literally 'crown of boasting'] in the presence of our Lord Jesus when he comes." This is even clearer. Notice he does not say, "they will receive a crown" or "I will receive a crown because of them." He says "*they are* our crown." This is remarkable. This is not the ruler's crown but the victor's crown, given to the winner of an athletic contest or to a soldier who had won a great victory or a civilian who was receiving honors for service to a city or state. The imagery is an athletic arena or field of battle, and Paul is receiving the laurel wreath or crown as the one who led them to victory. The "boasting," however, is not in his own achievement but in their own spiritual triumphs as brought about by the Lord. Paul's pride is in what God has done in them. The crown will be given at Christ's return, and the two, Paul and the Thessalonians, will share that crown.

So Paul concludes, "Is it not you? Indeed, you are our glory and joy." For the Romans, *doxa* primarily meant "fame," but for Christians it meant to be "honored" by God, to share his "glory." In this context it especially referred to eschatological glory ascribed them by Christ. This glory was already theirs in Christ, and at the same time they had not yet experienced it in its fullness. Paul as earlier is saying that the Thessalonians themselves are both glory and joy to him. The earthly side of this is seen in some translations: "You are our pride and joy." Yet this is much more than that, for both the glory and the joy are only partly experienced in the present, and we await a much deeper glory and joy when eternity begins.

## PAUL SENDS TIMOTHY ON A MISSION TO HELP THEM (3:1–5)

Paul's mission team was worried. They had been forced to leave too soon and hadn't had time to prepare these new believers to face the pressures arrayed against them. They had made more than one attempt to get back to them, but Satan had stymied each one. In light of the severe persecution and their ignorance of many theological truths, there was a real danger that Satan had overwhelmed them spiritually (v. 5b). So a short time earlier Paul had sent Timothy on a fact-finding mission (v. 5a) so he could strengthen them spiritually (v. 2).

### TIMOTHY SENT TO STRENGTHEN THEM (3:1–2)

They experienced a huge setback to their plans when Satan thwarted their every attempt to return, and their concerns could not be assuaged. So they were increasingly frustrated, and it built to a peak until "we could stand it no longer." They couldn't go back, and they didn't want to go forward with their mission plans (probably to Corinth) without knowing and doing their best to help the Thessalonians in their crisis of persecution. They cared so much for the Thessalonians and had to do *something*. The team decided that Silas and Timothy would remain in Berea, and Paul would go and be left by himself in Athens waiting for word (Acts 17:14–15).

The use of the plural "ourselves" is difficult since in Acts Paul went alone to Athens, asking that his associates come to him as soon as possible. Most agree that it refers to the collective decision that they made to have Paul go alone to Athens, and so we could translate, "we ourselves thought it best [that I] be left alone in Athens." A group of Berean believers accompanied him to Athens and then went back to Berea with instructions to the team to return to Paul ASAP. They apparently did so briefly, and Paul then sent Timothy to Thessalonica to encourage the believers there (v. 2). We are not told where, but Silas apparently went off on an errand (somewhere in Macedonia), leaving Paul alone in Athens. Timothy remained there some time, was quite successful, and then returned to Paul (who had by that time gone to Corinth) with the good news (3:6; Acts 18:5).

In verse 2 Timothy becomes the emissary of Paul to the Thessalonians. He is "sent," a term with theological depth meaning he is a designated "apostle" in the sense of a "sent one" (the meaning of *apostolos*) with Paul's authority behind him. Although he was young, he was very reliable and deeply sensitive to others (Phil 2:20), and Paul often sent him as his representative (1 Cor 4:17; 16:10; Phil 2:19). He labels him both a "brother and co-worker," the first to show he is a full member of the team and the second to show his office on the team. They knew Timothy well from the earlier mission, but still his youth could be an impediment, so Paul wants them to know he has full authority from Paul to represent him. He is fully a member of the team, which functions "in God's service[2] in spreading the gospel of Christ" and must be respected

---

2. The Greek is literally "God's coworker," and this has puzzled many. It is not that he is "God's companion" in ministry but more likely that he is Paul's coworker "for God" or "in God's service," thus the NIV translation.

as such. Paul is present with them in the person of Timothy, and he wants them to realize that.

His purpose was clear. He was being sent "to strengthen and encourage you in your faith." Each verb is important. "Strengthen" (*stērixai*) means to "shore up" or "make firm" a building or "establish" a movement or group. Paul was afraid Satan had shaken their faith and so wanted Timothy to make their faith firm and strong against all attempts to destroy it. The second verb, "encourage" (*parakalesai*), occurs throughout this letter (2:12; 3:2, 7; 4:1, 10, 18; 5:11, 14) and connotes both exhortation and encouragement or comfort. Here it is definitely the latter, and Paul is asking Timothy both to shore up their faith and comfort them in all the adversity they are experiencing at the hands of their persecutors.

It is specifically the "faith" of these new converts that needed strengthening, and Paul uses the word five times in 3:1–10. Their very trust in God was endangered by the severity of their trials. Not only that, but "faith" also refers to the content of what they believe and live for, the full reality of their new life in Christ (see also v. 5). Their new life in Christ as a whole was threatened, and Paul desperately wanted to get help to them through Timothy. That is a lot to saddle a young leader like Timothy with, and Paul showed a great deal of trust in him. We would expect Silas to be the one chosen, but Paul had to have his reasons. Timothy must have shown himself to be a young prodigy with enormous potential.

## THE DANGER THAT PERSECUTION BRINGS (3:3–4)

Paul now adds detail to the reason why he must send Timothy to them. What is endangering their faith is severe opposition and persecution. He does not want anyone to be "unsettled by these trials." The verb *sainesthai* only occurs here in the New Testament and originally referred to the wagging of a dog's tail. So it could refer to the idea of flattering a person, and in this sense it has been thought to connote opponents fawning over and flattering the Thessalonians, thereby leading them away from Christ. While that is possible, another option provides a better understanding. The wagging tail could picture an unstable person, unsettled in their faith. This fits the imagery better, as Timothy is to firm up their unsettled faith, stabilize them in the midst of their shaken spiritual condition.

What is shaking them is their intense suffering resulting from severe trials or afflictions noted often (1:6; 3:3-4, 7; 2 Thess 1:4, 6-7). Paul gives two qualifications. First, he says, "You know quite well that we are destined for them." They had been taught this before and so should be fully aware of this reality. Persecution is part of the divine will for his people. It should never come as a shock. "Destined" refers to what is divinely appointed, a necessary experience in a fallen world. Ironically, in Acts 14:22 this was taught to the believers just after Paul was stoned and left for dead in Lystra: "We must go through many hardships to enter the kingdom of God." So he knew this truth firsthand. The reality of rejection and opposition to the gospel truth is everywhere in the New Testament (e.g., Matt 5:11-12; John 16:33; Rom 8:17; 2 Cor 4:7-12; Heb 11:32-39; 1 Pet 3:13-17). The heresy of the gospel of prosperity is quite evident in these passages.

The second qualification is in verse 4, and it builds on the first. These converts should not be shaken by affliction because they have already been warned about it: "when we were with you, we kept telling you that we would be persecuted." The verb "kept telling you" is imperfect tense, which means on repeated occasions Paul and the others had stressed this reality. There could be no surprise when the "prophecy" came to pass. It was an important aspect of the catechetical instruction given new converts and was understood by all. We desperately need this in our day as well. We do not live in as hostile an environment as they did, though our society is becoming more anti-Christian by the day, but we need a "theology of suffering" whereby believers understand the place of trials in general in the Christian life. Persecution is a type of trial and like all suffering is meant to drive us to the Lord.

Not only was persecution predicted, it fulfilled itself and came to pass: "And it turned out that way, as you well know." Note the first-person plural "we" throughout. Paul wants them to know they aren't alone in their suffering. The mission team (indeed, all the saints) were being persecuted. So the destined suffering is real, and the Thessalonians "know" that. In fact, this discussion of persecution is framed with the fact that they "know" firsthand all about it (vv. 3b, 4b).

## The Reason for Sending Timothy (3:5)

In verses 3–4 Paul discussed the primary difficulty the Thessalonians were experiencing—persecution—and the second reason for sending Timothy to them, to shore up their unsettled faith. Now he returns to the topic of verses 1–2, his decision to send Timothy. So this decision frames the paragraph and becomes the primary emphasis. The Thessalonians are hurting because of the barrage of pressure heaped on them by their adversaries and need to be spiritually strengthened. For added stress, Paul switches from the plural "we" to the singular "I" so as to show them how anxious for them he is personally. "For this reason" shows that the sending is due to the trouble the afflictions have caused.

There is another reason why Timothy had to come: Paul's forced departure and absence from them (2:17–18). He had no access to them and was quite worried about the state of their walk with Christ under all the pressure. He repeats from verse 1 "when I could stand it no longer," meaning his concern for them was at the breaking point and he had to get some information. Therefore he was sending Timothy "to find out about your faith." In this context their "faith" isn't trust in Christ or the body of doctrine in which they believe. It refers to the full reality of their walk with Christ, all in which they have put their trust. Timothy is to test their faithfulness to Christ, to see if they have wavered in their allegiance to him.

Paul is afraid for them, fearing "that in some way the tempter had tempted you." The "tempter" is clearly Satan (2:18), the fallen angel (Rev 12:7–9) who is the primary adversary of God and his people, and works night and day and "leads the world astray" (Rev 12:9; 20:3). Here this is not just general temptation but Satan's primary purpose of turning people away from God and destroying their "faith." Paul identifies the severe persecution in Thessalonica in its true identity as the work of Satan. As they endure the opposition of the Jews and pagans, they are also engaging in spiritual warfare, and Paul is quite worried about how the battle is going.

Since Paul and his team are the spiritual parents of the Thessalonians (2:7, 11), he is also worried that their "labors might have been in vain," an empty effort and devoid of any results. The "labor" (1:3, 2:9) is the hard work and effort that went into proclaiming the gospel and evangelizing the Thessalonians. Satan was testing them to the limit, and since Paul had no access to discovering the true state of their faith, he worried quite a bit about the worst-case scenario, that they had given in to the pressure and deserted their faith. If that proved to be true, all the effort put into the Thessalonians would be for naught, useless. Paul loved those people deeply and just had to know. So he sent Timothy and waited for news, first in Athens and then in Corinth.

## TIMOTHY RETURNS WITH GOOD NEWS (3:6–10)

The wait had been a long one. The trip alone from Athens to Thessalonica was ten days at a minimum, and so the delay was excruciating for Paul. Yet in the end it was worth it. The old hymn is proved true, and Paul's fears are assuaged as Timothy returns with the news, "All is well with their soul!" Paul had wondered if they still returned his deep affection and care for them, and the answer was quite positive (v. 6), and his worries about the state of their walk with Christ are answered—they are rock solid in their faith (vv. 7–8). The news could not be any better, and Paul is overjoyed, longing to see them (vv. 9–10).

## GOOD NEWS ABOUT THEIR CONTINUED AFFECTION (3:6)

Finally, Timothy returns (with Silas, Acts 18:5). "Just now come" tells us that this letter was written shortly after that return. Paul had traveled to Corinth for the rest of the second missionary journey (Acts 18:1) and had been anxiously waiting for him. Since Silas was elsewhere in Macedonia, probably Philippi, they probably met on the way back and traveled together (we don't know if it was planned that way). I wish I could have been in Corinth for that meeting. Paul, filled with anxiety, fearing the worst, then exploding with joy as each bit of wondrous news took those fears completely away.

Paul mentions two aspects of that news. The first two terms, faith and love, relate to their spiritual state. Both are major terms in this letter, "faith" in 1:3, 8; 3:1–10 (five times); 5:8, and "love" in 1:3; 3:12; 4:9; 5:8, 13. So the Thessalonians were remaining faithful and growing in their Christian life. Far from caving in to the persecution, they were actually flourishing spiritually. The second aspect, their attitude toward Paul and his team, is also glowing: "you always[3] have pleasant memories of us and … long to see us." There were no bad feelings toward the team at the forced departure. They undoubtedly understood it was out of Paul's hands and refused to blame him for it. Indeed, they had nothing but "pleasant memories" of their short time together.

Even more, they couldn't wait to see them again. The verb itself (epipotheō) expresses an intense longing, a deep desire for a reunion. Paul often uses it when he is separated from someone he cares about and wants to be with them again (Rom 1:11; Phil 2:26). The team had long wanted the separation to end ("just as we also long to see you"), and to know the feelings are reciprocated is a huge relief. To know that the affection is mutual is just what Paul

---

3. "Always" comes between the two clauses and could go with either. While it could go with the following participle, "always longing to see us," it is better with the NIV to take it with the main verb, "always have pleasant memories."

needed to hear. We get a real feeling for the depths of Paul's love for others here. This is not a cold, uncaring leader but a loving, caring spiritual parent.

### GOOD NEWS ABOUT THEIR FIRM STANCE IN CHRIST (3:7-8)

Paul wants them to know what a relief the news was and how encouraged it made him: "in all our distress and persecution we were encouraged about you because of your faith." The ministry on the second missionary journey seemed like an endless litany of hard times and one time of persecution after another (Acts 16–18), from jail in Philippi to being forced to flee in Thessalonica and Berea, then ridicule and rejection in Athens. By the time he arrived in Corinth, he admitted that he was "in weakness with great fear and trembling" (1 Cor 2:3). God even sent him a vision, telling him, "Do not be afraid. ... For I am with you" (Acts 18:9-10). They were going through emotional "distress" and outward "persecution," and the combination was almost more than he could take. This was not helped by the lengthy wait for news from Timothy. So when it came, and when it was extraordinarily good news, he was, needless to say, overjoyed. He desperately needed comfort (see Rom 1:12; Phlm 7), and this news provided it.

To learn that their faith was indeed strong, and that all the adversity had served to strengthen it rather than dissipate it, was greatly encouraging and a model for all churches, as Paul has already said in 1:7. Several believe the terms "distress and persecution" are eschatological (in this case, better translated as "distress and affliction"), portraying the sufferings of the end times. However, there is nothing in the context to suggest this. Rather, he is showing that he is one with the Thessalonians in their own distress. He understands all they are going through, and he is thankful that they have comforted him in the same way he wishes to comfort them.

The result of it all is an exclamation of pure joy, "For now we really live." The encouragement of verse 7 turns to language of resurrection. There is strong emphasis on *nyn*, "now." Paul has been speaking of the past distress and all the pressure he was under. It is almost if he is saying he was slowly dying under it all. The *nyn* refers to the arrival of the good news from Timothy, which changed everything, and a new life began. Metaphorically, Paul had been in the Valley of Dry Bones, slowly wasting away to nothing. Now the relief is so great that it is as if the breath of life entered and rejuvenated him.

The reason for this spiritual resurrection event is the realization that "you are standing firm in the Lord." This clause is debated because the introductory particle is very unusual, not a causal conjunction but the conditional *ean* ("if"). However, that term normally takes the subjunctive case (the case of uncertainty, "might"), but for the only time in Paul, this time it uses the indicative (the case of reality, "is"). As a result, several scholars read it as a causal, namely "if, as is indeed the case" = "since." That could well be true, but I agree with those who see some conditional force, with a hortatory thrust that turns it into exhortation, "If, as you already are, you continue to stand firm in the Lord." Paul is renewed by their spiritual steadfast faith in extreme adversity, but at the same time he must exhort them to work even harder at their walk with Christ. His well-being in ministry is interconnected with their spiritual condition.

## HIS GREAT JOY AND DESIRE TO SEE THEM (3:9–10)

These two verses constitute a single sentence in the Greek centering on the great joy Paul feels because of them and his deep desire to see them again. Both parts are clothed with prayer and thankfulness to God. Paul continues his practice of thanking God regularly for these wonderful people (1:3; 2:19). He is completely aware that all the wonderful things that have taken place in this church are due to God's empowering presence, and so he asks, "How can we thank God enough for you?" Human language fails, and human efforts are inadequate to repay God for all the goodness he has done.

The language of reciprocity is somewhat unusual. The verb behind "in *return* for all the joy we have" is *antapodounai*, a verb used for repaying a debt and implying a total return of the amount owed. This is reminiscent of the psalmist who asks, "What shall I return to the LORD for all his goodness to me?" It is impossible to repay the largesse of God, and all that can be done is to live our lives in constant praise to God for his *chesed* and *emet* (his loving-kindness and faithfulness). The Lord has brought spiritual growth to the Thessalonians and joy to Paul, who wants to repay him for all he has done. Note the thanks is "for you," namely, their victorious faith (vv. 6, 7) and firm stance for Christ (v. 8). His expression of joy is linked to 2:19–20, "you are our glory and joy."

His point is that all the thanksgiving he could render is not enough to repay God for his intervention in the lives of the Thessalonians. Paul was indebted to God and did not have adequate resources for repaying that debt. The gift was just too magnificent. The hyperabundance of joy ("all the joy") is beyond their ability to reciprocate, and it is a joy they are experiencing "in the presence of our God," as they worship, both individually and corporately. This is where the "return" or repayment will have to take place. It is inadequate, but Paul and his team plan to lift up their hands and faces in worship and thanks to God for all he has done. That is the best they can do.

In verse 10 the prayers move from worship to petition and become constant ("night and day") and intense ("most earnestly") with the purpose "that we may see you again and supply what is lacking in your faith." The prayer to see them again is almost the major theme of the letter so far, and so the emphasis on both frequent and deep prayer is not mere conventional language but expresses his true feelings. He desperately wants to see them again and so is petitioning God with all the strength he has. He uses a strong verb, *deomai*, which means to "beg, implore, plead." The modifier is also emphatic, *hyperekperissou*, "beyond abundance, most earnestly." Paul wants them to know he is asking the Lord for a clear way to come to them with everything he has.

There are two prayer requests: first, a face-to-face reunion, and second, a fulfilling ministry with them. After the all-too-brief yet immensely successful founding time of evangelism, they had been ripped from these people and forced to flee to Berea (2:17; Acts 17:10), and from that time they were in limbo, waiting first in Athens and then in Corinth and looking for ways to get back to them (2:18; Acts 17:16; 18:1). So the desire to see them face to face (both 2:17 and here) was at the heart of everything. His earlier attempts were stymied by Satan (2:18), and he sent Timothy (3:1–2) to make up for it. Now once more Paul wants to come to them personally. Even this letter won't make up for personal contact. This is seen in the second request.

The necessity of a personal visit is to "supply what is lacking in your faith." Paul felt that only he could accomplish this. The verb *katartizō* is used for finishing the education of a student so they are ready for adulthood or restoring something to working order. So there is some area in the training of these new converts that Paul was unable to complete, and he needed to get back to them in order to finish the job. He is thrilled that they are firm and growing in their faith, but there is still a deficiency that must be corrected.

It is likely that Paul had in mind issues he addresses in the rest of this letter: purity and self-control in their sexual conduct (4:1–8), proper knowledge regarding the return of Christ and the fate of those who die in the Lord (4:13–5:10), and a group of "idlers" who were sponging off the rest of the church (5:14; 2 Thess 3:6–15). These things were "lacking" and needed to be corrected, and Paul felt his personal presence was needed to accomplish this. He is thrilled with their overall walk with the Lord, but there is still work to be done.

## PAUL PRAYS TO RETURN AND
## STRENGTHEN THEIR FAITH (3:11–13)

Paul discussed his earnest prayers to return in verse 10, and now he utters one of those constant prayers to conclude his discussion in 2:17–3:13. The theme throughout has been his great desire to see them again, so this provides a natural culmination. There are two parts, and they correspond to the two themes seen thus far, a prayer for God to clear the path for their return (v. 11) and a prayer for them for increasing love and spiritual strength (vv. 12–13).

### PRAYER FOR THEIR RETURN TO THE THESSALONIANS (3:11)

The first prayer stems from his concerns over his forced absence from them and his desire to see them again in 2:17–3:5 and 3:10. The mission of Timothy to them as Paul's representative certainly helped, but Paul feels a personal return is still mandated. The only way it can happen is for God to go before them and make it possible, and that is his prayer. He addresses it to "our God and Father himself"; the frequent mention of the fatherhood of God (1:1, 3; 3:13; 2 Thess 1:1, 2; 2:16) stresses his watchful care and protective presence. He is their *abba*, the father who loves them completely and unequivocally. Prayer provides the intimate connection that defines the family of God. The other recipient is "the Lord Jesus," which as in 1:1, 3, stresses his lordship over his creation. These two subjects (God and Jesus) govern a singular verb, thus implicitly presenting them as a single being and emphasizing Jesus as deity. Paul can be assured that the Triune Godhead has heard his prayers and will act to do what is best.

The prayer is for the Godhead to "clear the way for us to come to you," a construction metaphor that pictured a road or path with obstacles that had to be cleared before safe passage could take place. It was used metaphorically for following the right way or path as designated by God (Prov 4:26–27) and for God guiding his people to the correct path (Pss 5:8, 37:23). The verb is used this

same way in the prayer of 2 Thessalonians 3:5 and here is a petition that God will remove Satan's obstacles (2:18) and allow Paul
to get back to the Thessalonians. The Satanic obstructions will be
cleared out, and the way back to these beloved believers will be
cleared by divine action.

## PRAYER FOR THE STRENGTHENING OF THEIR LOVE AND THEIR HEARTS (3:12–13)

This prayer too builds on earlier concerns for their spiritual
strengthening (2:3–4) and again asks "the Lord" (abbreviated from
v. 11) to do what Paul in himself cannot do. In the first part Paul asks
that the Lord "make your love increase and overflow for each other
and for everyone else." They were already known for the depth of
their love for each other (1:3; 4:9–10), but there is always room to
grow. In 2 Thessalonians 1:3 this prayer was already answered as
"the love all of you have for one another is increasing." The two
verbs (*pleonasai, perisseusai*) are fairly synonymous, both meaning to "increase, grow, abound," and Paul combines them to give
it a superlative force, "increase to the uttermost." So "overflow-
ing" is a perfect choice.

This is a very important command for today. In the New
Testament the church is much more than just an assembly of
believers; it is both a community of people who share the faith
and a family who love and care deeply for one another. Let's ask
how extensively this last level is true in our churches. How many
come every Sunday but actually have few if any real friends in the
church? How many of us see each other socially on a regular basis?
We need genuine love in our churches, friends on whom we can
rely. I grew up with a complete emphasis on the spiritual, but I am
more and more realizing how critical the social is in our churches.

Elsewhere in Thessalonians the stress is on their internal love
for each other, but here Paul adds "and for everyone else." There
are three levels of love in Scripture—love for God, for brothers and
sisters in Christ, and for humanity as a whole. It may be this third

sense that is "lacking in your faith" and needs to be "completed" (v. 10). "Everyone else" must mean unbelievers, probably including the very ones who are persecuting them, as in "love your enemies" in Matthew 5:43–48. Paul states it quite well in Romans 12:14: "Bless those who persecute you," and Galatians 6:10, "Do good to all people, especially to those who belong to the family of believers." If the church is to engage in mission to the lost, they must learn to be known for their love. "Love your neighbor" (Lev 19:18) is a key mandate that must govern external relationships (Matt 22:39; Rom 13:8–10; Gal 5:14–15; Jas 2:8).

This love for each other and for all has a concrete example— "just as ours does for you." The love and compassion of the mission team for the new believers was obvious and clear and actually adds a fourth level of love to those above in the previous paragraph. This is part of the imitation theme I discussed in 1:6–7—"imitate our love for you as we imitate Christ's love for us." This is also similar to 3:6, "you long to see us, just as we also long to see you."

The final element of Paul's prayer centers on their spiritual state and the ethical conduct that flows out of it (v. 13). In 3:2 he said he was sending Timothy to "strengthen … your faith," and in 3:10 he said he wanted to return to them in order to "supply what is lacking in your faith." This is now the second thing lacking (after helping their love to grow in v. 12). As their love increases in depth, it will "strengthen your hearts" and enable them to be "blameless and holy" as they live the Christian life in a sin-sick world.

In 3:2 the strengthening is in the present, to anchor them in Christ and enable them to remain spiritually secure in Christ. Here the strength has a future orientation, to enable them to overcome the pressures of the age (sexual in 4:3–8) and live blameless, holy lives and to do so in light of that final day of reckoning, the last judgment. I will develop these themes below, and they will dominate the rest of the letter, holiness in 4:1–12 and the return of Christ and final judgment in 4:13–5:10. The first theme, holiness, is found in the prayer that at that final day they "will be found blameless in holiness" (NIV "blameless and holy") as they stand "in the presence of our God and Father."

The two terms were also found together in 2:10 to describe how "blameless and righteous and holy" Paul's team was when they founded the church. They mean the same here, depicting that exemplary moral behavior that glorifies God and lives victoriously above the pressures of the world. So he is asking the Thessalonians to emulate that conduct they saw in the lives of their founding fathers in the faith. As such this looks forward to 4:3–8 and details the kind of life that must be characteristic of them in the future leading up to that moment when they stand before God in that blameless, holy persona that has defined their earthly existence. God's people have always been called to holiness, beginning at Sinai when they were labeled a "holy nation" (Exod 19:6) and called in the Sinai covenant to remain so (Deut 7:6; 19:6). The Thessalonians as part of the new people of God, the new Israel, are called to that same lifestyle. When they stand before the throne and give account for their lives, they need to be found blameless and separate from the world, totally given over to God.

Paul defines the final judgment in two ways here, first by the reminder that they will stand "in the presence of our God and Father" at his judgment seat (Rom 14:10; 2 Cor 5:10). This title has appeared already in the beginning of this prayer at 3:11, reminding them of the intimate relationship of God as the loving Father who watches over his children. Here the Father is Judge (1 Pet 1:17; see 4:6) at his great white throne (Rev 20:11–15).

God will be the eschatological Judge at that culminating event of world history "when our Lord Jesus comes with all his holy ones." Paul is truncating these events together as part of the eschaton, or "end" of the world. In actuality, when we put it all together, an entire series of events constitute that End event. Christ will come, and at that moment the saints will receive their resurrection bodies and follow the Lord to the destruction of the antichrist and forces of evil. Then will ensue the millennial reign (depending on one's view of this event), and the final judgment will take place at the culmination of all these events and at the beginning of eternity (Rev 20:11–15 leading into 21:1–22:5). Paul brings them together to make his point. Holiness must be our defining characteristic when we stand before the Lord at that final judgment.

When the Lord returns he is accompanied "with all his holy ones." There is wide disagreement whether this refers to the holy saints or the holy angels. There is no question that the angels of heaven will return with Christ, and Zechariah 14:5 pictures the angels when "the Lord my God will come, and all the holy ones with him" (see also Jude 14). Angels are often called "holy ones" (Job 5:1; 15:15; Ps 89:7; Dan 8:13), and it is clear they will be present at the return of Christ (Matt 16:27; 25:31; 2 Thess 1:7; Rev 19:14). However, many are convinced these are the "saints" (= "holy ones," Paul's use everywhere in his writings), which would reinforce the emphasis on holiness here. All in all, it is a difficult decision, but it seems better to see the biblical idea of the angels as the armies of heaven accompanying the Lord here and as "holy ones" becoming another model for these believers to copy.

―――――

This is the concluding section of the first half of the letter, and so Paul draws together his concerns and hopes for the situation at Thessalonica. We must remember that Paul and his mission team had arrived after a very tumultuous time in Philippi and had an initial wondrous ministry in Thessalonica, winning converts and beginning to establish the church there. However, way too soon severe persecution broke out, and they were forced to flee to Berea, eventually sending Timothy to get news and waiting in Athens, then Corinth for his return.

As I have been saying all along, there is a **paraenetic** flavor in all of this, as Paul is using these circumstances as an example of what Christians regularly experience. So we are to take these circumstances and apply them to similar problems we face in life. Paul's forced separation from the Thessalonians and the obstacles Satan set up to destroy the work of God there (2:17–18) parallel times we pass through when Satan brings discouraging barriers into our ministry attempts. We too must not allow despair to take over but bring these difficulties before the Lord with the cautious optimism of prayer. The remarkable sequence of 2:19–20 is a capstone for this. God wants to bring victory and joy out of the struggles we all experience. The very people in whose lives we are investing become our reward and crown, for we share in their glory, and their victory provides an eternal reward for us.

The mission of Timothy (3:1–5) to discover the state of the believers in Thessalonica and to settle them down spiritually and strengthen them in the Lord has great potential as a model for ministry today. Mainly, it demonstrates a deep, loving concern for those God has placed under our care. Paul could not rest until he knew the true state of these dear friends. He had been forced to leave way too soon and wanted Timothy to be his ambassador to them. This deep love and involvement with those to whom we minister should be the hallmark of every church and Christian organization. At every level those in charge must be "in love" with those people they serve.

The news when it finally came (3:6–10) seemed miraculous and brought intense joy and thankfulness with it. Like Paul we must learn to wait on the Lord and be patient for his time in working out everything for the best (Rom 8:28). As in Hebrews 11 this lesson and its results will sometimes take a lifetime to learn, but God is at work and oversees every crisis we experience. The message here, as in the book of Acts, is that all our difficulties are actually an opportunity to watch the Spirit work, and God will never let us down. Like Paul's distress drove him, our distress must drive us to trust the Lord more deeply, and so more pressure simply means more prayer, as we intercede constantly and more and more deeply (v. 10) for God to do his work.

The final element of the section (3:11–13), as we would expect, is a prayer that culminates it all in which Paul lifts his two main concerns of the first half of the letter once more before the Lord: his desire to return for them and his concern that they grow stronger in the Lord. Prayer does two things: it channels more of God and his empowering presence into a situation, and it draws us even more completely into that dependence on God that is the mainstay of all spiritual victory. Paul never stopped praying these key concerns and leaving them with the Lord. It is that continued, intense prayer that brings results, and it provides an exceedingly practical model for us.

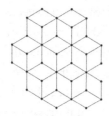

# THE HOLY LIFESTYLE
# THAT PLEASES GOD
(4:1–12)

W̶e now enter the central part of the letter, 4:1–5:22, where Paul seeks to "supply what is lacking in your faith" (3:10) and address concerns he was unable to address because he was forced to flee to Berea too soon (Acts 17:10). He has finished explaining his absence and the events during that time, and he is now ready to dive into the real needs of these people. He still has hopes that he will be able to come back and get into these issues face to face (3:11), but they cannot wait and he has to address them now in the letter. Undoubtedly these particular issues arose in Timothy's report, and Paul takes them one at a time, beginning with issues of holiness—sexual conduct (4:3–8) and brotherly love (4:9–12)— then turning to **eschatology**—the fate of those who die in Christ (4:13–18) and the meaning of the Day of the Lord (5:1–11)—and finishing with final instructions for church life (5:12–22).

## PAUL DISCUSSES LIVING SO AS
## TO PLEASE GOD (4:1–2)

Paul here provides an introduction to the whole section, detailing the kind of lifestyle acceptable and pleasing to the Lord. For "we instructed you how," the Greek reads, "just as you received from

us how you must walk and please the Lord." This is semi-technical language for the reception of official catechetical instruction
(see 2:13, where it also occurs), so it is fairly formal and refers
to very important ethical instruction. Oh, that Christians today
would consider it as deeply important to walk so as to please the
Lord! There seems to be a moral chasm developing in many seg-
ments of the church. I once talked to a group of youth pastors, who
shared with me that one of the greatest problems is the number
of kids from supposedly strong Christian homes who know what
the Bible teaches but just don't care. That kind of person is harder
to reach than the dedicated atheist.

Paul wants his readers to be very serious in their desire to live
the Christian life so as to please God. For emphasis he uses two
similar verbs, "ask" and "urge" or "exhort" them to action. Both
verbs contain the idea of beseeching or imploring them to proper
conduct. Scholars call this an "appeal formula," and it is used in
letters of friendship to gently instruct disciples who are open and
ready for teaching. This entreaty, however, does not merely come
with the authority of Paul behind it. They are exhorted "in the
Lord Jesus"—the authority of the Lord of the universe is behind
it. Paul clearly wants them to understand how central and critical this is for the Christian life. It is not to be taken lightly but is
at the heart of virtually everything. In fact, this Christ-centered
authority will come up again in verse 2 (and several more times
in succeeding verses) to anchor it firmly in their consciousness.

The command itself is worded strongly: "received from us how
you must walk and please God" (HCSB). The divine "must" (dei)
makes this a necessity, not an option. The two verbs should be
translated, "walk in such a way that you please God." As in 2:12,
the "walk" is the way we live the Christian life and conduct ourselves according to God's demands. The second is the purpose of
the first, "live so as to please God." The idea of pleasing God is central to both testaments (Num 23:27; Pss 19:14; 104:34; Rom 12:1–2;
Eph 5:10). In this letter it is positive in 2:4 ("we are not trying to

please people but God") and negative in 2:15 (the Jews "displease God"). To please God is to be acceptable to him.

Paul asks that they not only make this a priority but also "increase" or "abound" (*perisseuō*) in it "more and more." This is another superlative. It is not enough to simply seek to please God. They need to grow exponentially in conduct that is pleasing to God, making certain that more and more areas of their lives are subordinated to his will. This is true holiness, as one aspect of your life after another comes under the rubric of divinely led conduct.

Throughout this letter Paul has stressed that the Thessalonians already "know" certain points he is making (1:4, 5; 2:1–2, 5, 11; 3:3–4). By having them recall the previous teaching, he reinforces its message and power in their lives. This is what he does here (v. 2), saying, "For you know what instructions we gave you by the authority of the Lord Jesus." In fact, this reinforces a point made in verse 1, that they had already "received" the instruction "from us" (NIV "we instructed you"). So there is a threefold stress (you received, you know, we gave you) on the crucial fact that the teaching of this section is in continuity with the official catechetical truths of the church, which stem from the gospel itself as revealed by Christ.

This is a strongly worded statement. The term for "instructions" is *parangelias*, an emphatic term for "commands" that was used for the orders of a military officer or a government official, which had to be obeyed or else (also used in 1 Tim 1:5, 18; see also 2 Tim 2:3–4). Not only are the commands absolute, but they arrive under "the authority of the Lord Jesus." Note the progression of authority—from the Lord of all, to the gospel/apostolic proclamation, to catechetical instruction, to local transmission, to living out these truths in daily life. Paul's entire emphasis is on the necessity of obedience. These are not optional teachings. This will be critical in verses 3–8, where we learn of an instance in which many of the Thessalonians were willingly disobedient (v. 8 below). Paul certainly intended that verses 1–2 prepare specifically for this issue.

There is an important lesson in this: when we encounter teachers who claim "brand-new insight" in their messages, we must be extremely leery of what they say. There are what we often label "new" truths, though these are actually deeper understanding and exegetical "insights" into the received truths. For instance, our knowledge of Bible backgrounds has at least quadrupled in the last fifty years, and we know so much more about the meaning of what is written in biblical books. (I am trying to incorporate many of these in this very commentary!) But we have not *changed* the doctrines taught in it, just deepened our understanding of what is already there. Books are constantly being published on the Trinity or on substitutionary atonement, but not new doctrines about the meaning of our salvation. There have been innumerable works on the meaning of atonement, but they have not changed the fact that we are saved because Jesus paid the price and shed his blood on the cross for the forgiveness of our sins.

## SANCTIFICATION MEANS AVOIDING SEXUAL IMMORALITY (4:3–8)

Apparently these new believers had faithfully sought to follow what they had been taught. But there was one area where many of them could not yield to the ways of Christ: sexual conduct. Holiness does not just mean separation from the things of the world. It also demands purity of conduct, practicing what pleases God (v. 1). Those who truly belong to God cannot practice that which is contrary to his will, and several in their church were doing just that. The emphasis in nearly every verse of this section is that these commands come not from Paul but from God himself.

The sexual mores of the Greco-Roman world are well known. Liaisons outside of marriage were not considered wrong. In fact, it was more than tolerance; such assignations were actually expected for "well-rounded" men. Marriages tended to be arranged, with the men somewhat established in business and in their mid-twenties while the women were in their teens. Marriages were for status and family connections, so most believed that women were to be faithful to their husbands while husbands were free to add pleasure outside the marriage bed. Female slaves were the property of their owner, and one of their duties was to satisfy the owner when he wished.

The wife bore children and managed the home, while concubines and mistresses brought pleasure into his life. One exception was the wives of other men, but many Romans turned a blind eye to that restriction as well. Wives were expected to be tolerant and forgiving. In fact, in many circles promiscuity was inherent to Roman religion, with sexual congress part of the worship celebration. In Thessalonica, in the cults of Dionysus and Aphrodite phallic symbols dominated, and participants engaged in sexual license during the services. It has been said also that some temples had temple prostitutes for the pleasure of the attenders.

This permissive attitude made it very difficult for new believers to understand the sexual restrictions of Christianity. They had never conceived or heard of such a narrow attitude and so took a while to understand, let alone accept it. Those who surrendered to the Christian demands would have been ridiculed by their neighbors. Peter says it very well: "They are surprised that you do not join them in their reckless, wild living, and they heap abuse on you" (1 Pet 4:4). That some would surrender to the pressure and return to their old lifestyle should shock no one. This is the atmosphere Paul is writing to.

## Thesis: God Demands Holiness in Sexual Practices (4:3)

Paul had everything I have just said and more in his mind as he penned these opening words. For him, two preliminary issues were involved: the will of God and the meaning of sanctification as defining what should guide the process of the Christian walk. Clearly, it is conduct according to the will of God that alone can please God, and this conduct produces holy living. This can well be called the central motif in biblical ethics, for every aspect of

Christian behavior and lifestyle comes under the rubric of sanctification. From the Holiness Code of Leviticus 17–26, holiness became the defining mark for the lives of God's people. Moreover, the guiding force in biblical ethics is the will of God, so this opening statement is virtually a definition of it. This provides one of the critical aspects of biblical ethics. Combining this with verse 1, Paul is saying that immorality displeases God and results in his wrath, the sign of his displeasure.

The general truth is, "It is God's will that you should be sanctified," and sanctification in this case means "that you should avoid sexual immorality." A critical part of holy living is purity, the avoidance of all behavior that sullies your life in the sight of God. The term chosen is *hagiasmos*, with the *-mos* suffix stressing a passive force, "to be made holy," thereby bringing out the process by which God makes us pure and holy before him. Immorality disrupts that process and renders it null and void.

This was perhaps the most difficult area of ethical behavior for the early church, mainly because immorality was so pervasive and universally accepted in the Greco-Roman world. In the Jerusalem decree after the council of Acts 15, the only ethical aspect mentioned by the leaders of the church for Gentile converts was to "abstain from sexual immorality" (Acts 15:20, 29) because it was so hard to overcome. It was virtually ingrained into their mindset and so much a part of their way of life that it took a great deal of time and effort to break the habit. That is also why Paul has to take extensive time to deal with it here. The term here is *porneia*, a general word referring to any form of sexual behavior outside of marriage, not just adultery but homosexuality, pederasty, and so on.

Since throughout the Old Testament holiness was the key concept dividing Jew and Gentile and a defining characteristic of God's people separating them from the Gentiles, it is also critical that Paul uses it here. The simple fact that he does so demonstrates the new era that Christ has instituted. The Gentile converts have now joined believing Jews as the people of God, the new Israel, and an entirely "new covenant" period is here.

## THREE ATTENDANT COMMANDS (4:4–6A)

For full clarity on the issue, Paul gives three further orders that serve to flesh out what he is saying in more detail. He desires a full understanding of what he means by "avoid sexual immorality" and so explains three aspects of this divine demand.

(1) "Learn to control your own body in a way that is holy and honorable." This is the most difficult verse so far, and in most recent commentaries it demands a lengthy and very complex discussion. I will try to bring clarity to it if possible. The key is two terms, "vessel" (*skeuos*) and "control" (*ktasthai*). The first can refer to the human body, to one's wife (1 Pet 3:7, "weaker vessel"), or even to the male sexual organ (a real possibility here). The verb can refer to "controlling" or "acquiring" a thing. Putting these together, three interpretive options have appeared (seen in the NIV textual notes): (1) controlling your own body (or sexual organ); (2) learning to live with your wife in harmony; (3) acquiring a wife (rather than living in lust, see 1 Cor 7:9, "better to marry than to burn with passion"). Each of these is accepted by several interpreters.

However, in light of 1 Corinthians 7 and this context, the best of the three is the first, for it explains more of the issues here. The only way to defeat the immoral tendencies we all have is to gain "control" over our own bodies and refuse to do certain things (for instance, looking at pornographic websites, lusting at the beach, or watching the parade of beautiful people go by). A good argument can be made for a specific interpretation of "vessel" as the male sex organ, but the more general "body" makes more sense here. Control of one's self is seen throughout the New Testament (Acts 21:25; 1 Cor 6:9–10, 18, 7:2–9; Eph 5:3; Col 3:5; 1 Pet 2:11; Rev 21:8) as the best way to defeat promiscuous thoughts.

The way to gain control according to Paul is to do so "in a way that is holy and honorable." This is the positive side, with the negative in the next verse. Holiness of course is the defining idea of this entire section, beginning in verse 3. It is the complete antithesis of immoral thoughts and actions and here means gaining power over and defeating sexual desires. Its definition as "separation from the world to God" has special application to immoral behavior as the opposite of God-centeredness. Honor in a Greco-Roman setting was that behavior that received respect and praise from those around. In a Christian setting it is oriented especially to receiving praise from God. Immoral conduct is dishonorable because it treats others without respect as sexual objects and as such will bring God's wrath down upon you.

(2) "Not in passionate lust like the pagans" (v. 5): This is obviously part of the command in verse 4, but I am treating it as a separate command due to its importance. This is why it was so difficult for new Gentile converts to escape the pattern of temptation, lust, and immoral behavior they had inherited from their entire culture, and this is why it is just as hard today to overcome these sinful thoughts. Temptation to lust has never been so pervasive as it is today. Several divas have become multimillionaires not by acting or singing prowess but merely by displaying their bodies in myriad suggestive ways.

Paul's language is quite strong. The Greek is actually "the passion of lust," with the first term (*pathos*) referring to strong desire or passion that is addictive and gains control over one's thought life. The second term (*epithymia*) is a near synonym of the first, and together "passionate lust" is a perfect translation, as is its obverse, "lustful passions." The mindset is under the control of erotic passions, and the person has in a real sense "lost his mind" to those promiscuous thoughts.

The "pagans" are of course those who inhabit the non-Christian world and "do not know God." This ignorance of God (deliberate according to Rom 1:18–32) is the reason why they are under the control of sexual passions. The readers used to belong to that group but have found Christ and attained salvation. They are no

longer part of the heathen world, and holiness means you are forever "separate" from that world. Its practices will never again be
for you, and they should be abhorrent to true believers. Of course,
they are not, for the "flesh" or the tendency to sin in every one of
us is always drawn to that ungodly conduct. The only way to rise
above such passions is to know God and be driven by the desire
to please him in every area, especially that of sexual ethics. That
alone gives us the strength to control our bodies.

(3) "In this matter no one should wrong or take advantage of a
brother or sister" (v. 6a): Some have understood Paul to be changing his focus here and addressing commercial or business dealings
in which members defrauded ("take advantage") of others, but that
is extremely improbable because the whole of verses 3–8 centers
on sexual sins. "In this matter" has to mean the matter of sexual
sin. This refers to a sexual predator who is willing to use trickery
and deception to seduce another person. It could also refer to those
willing to break even Roman boundaries of propriety regarding
sex with a member of one's own household or a neighbor's spouse
or in this case a Christian "brother or sister." As many have said,
these are "illicit sexual affairs" in which people are wronged. The
sexual addict is willing to break societal rules to engage in immoral
pleasure. This is the complete opposite of the "honor" that should
be attendant in all sexual relationships according to verse 4.

## THE COMING JUDGMENT OF CHRIST (4:6B)

It is interesting that in this instance Paul has as final Judge "the
Lord" Jesus rather than God.[1] It is possible that part of the reason
is his desire to bring in a trinitarian emphasis, as God the Father
is the focus of verse 7, and the Holy Spirit of verse 8. The Greek

---

1. Some see "Lord" as referring to God here as well, since he is the eschatological Judge of Revelation 20:11–15. However, "Lord" throughout this letter
refers to Jesus (1:1, 3, 6, 8, and others), and Jesus often in Paul institutes judgment when he comes (Rom 12:19; Col 3:3–5; 1 Thess 5:1–11).

actually says "the Lord is avenger [*ekdikos*] with respect to all those who commit such sins." This is not just the judge who sentences lawbreakers but the civic official who punishes them as well. As "Lord" over his creation, Jesus is both Judge and Punisher who executes divine "vengeance" (the cognate term) on those who commit such egregious sins against not only those who are seduced but also against God. The justice and righteousness of God demand such harsh reprisal, for the sin itself is serious. People today think it nothing to act out all one's sexual fantasies. There is a moral vacuum that has consumed our society, and we must do a better job of addressing it.

Paul is probably looking forward to the final judgment, when the Lord Christ will carry out this judgment, although certainly Paul would see also a preliminary wrath that begins in the here and now. God's displeasure is present as well as future. There is a common misunderstanding today that God through the cross of Christ has already forgiven all our sins, future as well as past. However, this ignores the extensive teaching on the fact that we all will stand before the throne of Christ and give account for our lives (Rom 14:10; 2 Cor 5:10; Rev 22:12). Christians cannot sin with impunity and get away with anything they do. There are consequences. The Bible does not specify them, but the fact of judgment is too extensive to ignore. Remember, Paul is writing this warning to Christians, not non-Christians.

He adds to the warning, "as we told you and warned you before." He has in mind not just teaching about sexual sin but also teaching about the judgment seat of God and Christ. He had given them extensive instruction before he was forced to leave them. They knew this doctrine. The "warning" is a strong term referring to a solemn, emphatic notice about sexual sin and the judgment facing those who ignored the clear teaching of Scripture and the church against it. Those who ignored these warnings and flaunted their so-called freedom would pay dearly for their folly.

## CONCLUDING THOUGHTS (4:7–8)

Verse 7 functions as a summary of what Paul has said thus far and frames the passage with thoughts of sanctification/purity (vv. 3, 7–8). The idea of the call to salvation and the Christian life is what anchors these letters. The first leads directly into the second. The election to salvation involves the call to live out that salvation in daily life. In 1:4 the believer is chosen to belong to God, and in 2:12 they are called "into his kingdom and glory." The call involves by definition the call to sanctified living, to "live lives worthy of God" (2:12). In 5:23, the God who calls is the God who will "sanctify you through and through." And here that sanctifying process means the purity of living "a holy life." The object of God's call is salvation in Christ; the purpose[2] of God's call is holy living.

Impurity can be ceremonial, as in purity laws like eating foods that render you unclean or touching a corpse. This, however, refers to moral impurity (*akatharsia* can also be translated "unclean"). Paul is saying that God did not call them to be his children so they could practice sexual immorality and be impure. Holiness does not allow such conduct. To "live a holy life," one must eschew all such practices and embrace sexual purity. Then that life will be pleasing to God (4:1) and worthy of him (2:12).

In verse 8 Paul sets forth the implications of rejecting his message. Throughout this letter the emphasis is on God as the source of everything Paul says. His teachings stem first from God and then from the traditions of the church received from God. The "instructions" on sexual matters came "by the authority of the Lord Jesus" (v. 2) and by "God's will" (v. 3). Therefore, Paul concludes, "anyone who rejects this instruction does not reject a human being but God." Those who disobey will face the divine Judge, the Lord

---

2. I agree with those who say that the force of the preposition *epi* ("not for impurity") is purposive.

Christ, who will "punish" the disobedient (v. 7). This could not be a more serious matter.

The verb Paul chooses is *atheteō*, and it means to "set aside" or willfully ignore, thus to emphatically reject a command. So these people were not ignorant when they ignored the new set of moral mandates. These were people who showed contempt for the rules and in Old Testament language "sinned with a high hand" (i.e., deliberately). What Paul is saying is that when they disregard the injunctions of verses 3–6a, they are not merely refusing the views of the man Paul, but of the God who revealed these truths to him.

Moreover, the one they are rejecting is the giving God, and what he gives is not just ethical and moral orders but the Holy Spirit, whose presence enables one to have the strength to obey the mandates and gain control over their bodies (v. 4). The Spirit is given by God at conversion (Rom 8:11, 14–17) and empowers the saint so they can live victoriously in an evil world. The key text is Ezekiel 36:25–27, the prophecy where God promised to "put a new spirit in you," by which he meant, "I will put my Spirit in you and move you to follow my decrees and be careful to keep my laws." This was the key to the restoration of God's people to himself as the core to the new covenant age. Paul likely has Ezekiel in mind here.

The Greek wording accomplishes two things here. It alludes to Ezekiel 36 by stating that God gives the Holy Spirit "into [*eis*] you," thus linking it with Ezekiel's "I will put my Spirit in you." In addition, it takes the title "Holy Spirit" and highlights his holiness, "his Spirit who is holy," for the sake of the emphasis on holiness/sanctification in verses 1–8. When the Spirit enters us at conversion, the process of sanctification begins and the Spirit starts to make us holy. So for the believer to openly engage in sexual immorality also entails a rejection of the Spirit. However, Paul's emphasis is on the positive side here. The indwelling Spirit is here to give us the inner strength to gain control over our sex drive. On our own we are inadequate to stem the tide of immoral behavior. But we are not on our own. We are the new Israel, the covenant people of God, and we have the Spirit within.

## PAUL TEACHES ABOUT LOVE
## AND SOLITUDE (4:9–12)

The rest of the major section here is controlled by "Now about" (*peri de*), which occurs here and in 5:1, with just *de* introducing 4:13. Paul also uses this phrase in 1 Corinthians to designate the questions of a letter sent to him, with Paul's discussion there following the order of the letter's questions (1 Cor 7:1, 25; 8:1, 4; 12:1; 16:1, 12). So many think the Thessalonians have sent a letter with Timothy, and Paul is responding to its contents here. However, Paul mentions no such letter, and it is just as likely that Timothy has brought with him a series of questions from them for Paul. So the order of topics in 4:1–5:22 (probably including the sexual issue of 4:3–8) is in response to these questions. So the issue of brotherly love stems from their query.

### Love for One Another in the Church (4:9–10)

"Love for one another" is *philadelphia* ("brotherly love"), used mainly for the brothers and sisters of nuclear families and so emphasizing anew the central metaphor of the church as the family of God. This is seen in his use of infants (2:7), nursing mother (2:7), father (2:11), orphan (2:17), and brothers/sisters (1:4; 2:1, 9, 14, 17; 3:7; 4:1, 10, 13; 5:1, 4, 12, 14, 25, 26, 27) to picture the family togetherness of the church. So in a sense this culminates the idea of family love as the binding twine of God's people. This was a new concept in the ancient world, for love language tended to be restricted more to parent-child and sibling relationships. The church turned that around with its idea of the people of God as children of God and brothers and sisters of one another. So the Thessalonians were feeling their way through the issues.

Several times in this letter already Paul has lauded their community love. In 1:3 he spoke of "your labor prompted by love"; in 3:6 Timothy's report spoke of their "faith and love"; and in 3:12 Paul prayed that their love might "increase and overflow for each other and for everyone else." In fact, the depth of their love was well-known throughout Macedonia (4:10a). This section builds on the prayer of 3:12, especially the "[love] more and more" aspect (4:10b). With all this, we don't know for certain why there was a query about the loving relations in the assembly. It could have been tensions due to the members engaging in sexual license or debates over the eschatological issues of 4:13–5:11. I think it may have been due to the "idlers" of 5:14; 2 Thessalonians 3:6–15, but we cannot know for certain.

Paul interestingly says that about this "we do not need to write to you." He hardly means he has nothing to say or does not want to be asked such a question. He means they are already paradigms of the loving church and that God had already revealed these truths to them: "for you yourselves have been taught by God to love each other." The term used is unique in the Greek language (*theodidaktoi*), and many think Paul created the word himself to stress that all truth begins with God and has its true source in him. It is a deliberate allusion to Isaiah 54:13, "All your children will be taught by the LORD." The idea is also central to the new covenant prophecy in Jeremiah 31:34: "No longer will they teach their neighbor ... because they will all know me." God had awakened love, a fruit of the Spirit (Gal 5:22), in these naturally loving people, but this could also mean that the Lord revealed this to the church and that the Thessalonians had not only learned it but also put it into practice. Either way, Paul is commending them as models of a loving church.

In verse 10 Paul takes this point further: "And in fact, you do love all of God's family throughout Macedonia." This is exactly the point he has just made: these dedicated people have not only been taught how to love by God but also demonstrated it practically by extending that love throughout the province. Amazingly, these new converts already understand that not only are local believers brothers and sisters but all believers are. They are extending the grace and love of God universally. Paul doesn't say how they showed this love—possibly through the good works of Galatians 6:10 ("do good to all") or through hospitality to travelers or financial help like the collection for the poor Paul took to Jerusalem (2 Cor 8–9). This latter would make sense in a poverty-stricken province (2 Cor 8:2).

In keeping with 4:1, even though their community love is extensive, Paul urges that they "do so more and more." It is impossible to show too much love. He had already asked this in 3:12, "May the Lord make your love increase and overflow for each other and for everyone else." He asks for an increase qualitatively (in depth of feelings) and quantitatively (to everyone). In 4:1 they were to abound in conduct that pleased God, and now Paul mentions one of the primary areas where they will please God: in showing love to those around them.

## THE NEED FOR SELF-SUFFICIENT CHRISTIANS IN THE CHURCH (4:11–12)

This is a very difficult passage in terms of its meaning and place in the situation of the Thessalonian churches. Let me note three different interpretations: (1) Many link Paul's words here with 5:14 and 2 Thessalonians 3:6–15 and a group that had come to expect Jesus to return at any minute and so had stopped working to welcome him when he arrived. This forced the rest of the church to feed and take care of them, and Paul called them "idlers" (5:14). (2) Others link this with the patronage system of the Greco-Roman world, with clients who were completely dependent economically on a wealthy "patron" to whom they owed honor and allegiance. These people were more politically active than they were Christian and needed to withdraw and live quietly. (3) Another popular view is to understand this more generally as a call to pull back from their public image, stop getting involved in civic issues ("mind your own business"), and simply live quietly as believers. The severe opposition they have faced from outsiders was due in part to the high profile many of them kept. So to minimize the persecution, they needed to minimize their public persona.

The key is whether this passage is connected to 5:14 and 2 Thessalonians 3:6–15. If not, the more general understanding is correct. Personally, with the added "work with your hands" in verse 11, I think that the link is there, so I prefer the first understanding. These extreme end-of-the-world types were becoming a huge burden to the more responsible Christians and giving a bad name to Christianity among outsiders. They had to be dealt with and not allowed to live so selfishly off others.

Paul has three comments in his address to the situation. All flow out of the appeal to show more and more love to one another in verses 9–10:

1. "Make it your ambition to lead a quiet life": This means to "endeavor" or "aspire" and describes a strong desire to attain a certain thing, here a quiet life. On the surface this might mean a desire for solitude and peace, but that is unlikely. These idlers had been making a big splash in public and caused all kinds of trouble for the church. Their idleness had led them to meddle in the affairs of others and bring their wrath down on the church. Paul wants the church to have a high profile in evangelistic activity but a low profile in civic affairs. He is asking them to quit stirring up problems for the church by pushing the wrong agendas.

2. "Mind your own business": This is intimately connected with the quiet life and tells how one achieves it. It condemns the busybody meddling that characterized these people (2 Thess 3:11). There is a huge difference between the kind of loving concern that leads a person to admonish another for sinful or dangerous behavior and the busybody who meddles and gossips about others. The difference

is the love of verses 9–10. The busybody doesn't actually care about the other and just wants to meddle for entertainment's sake.

3. "Work with your hands, just as we told you": This tells us that most of the new converts were in the artisan class, as the upper class looked with disdain at those who soiled their hands with work. Still, this certainly addresses the idlers of 5:14 (= 2 Thess 3:10, "unwilling to work"), as they were giving the church a bad reputation as lazy, shiftless people. This constituted exploitation of others when they force them to show their love by taking care of these lazy bums. Note the parallel in Ephesians 4:28: "Anyone who has been stealing must steal no longer, but must work, doing something useful with their own hands." These idlers were in this sense "stealing" from the others by forcing them to take care of their needs. Paul had told them about this previously, probably when he was with them as founding pastor before the outbreak of persecution.

The purpose of these instructions ("so that," v. 12) is twofold. Externally, "your daily life may win the respect of outsiders." Internally, "you will not be dependent on anyone." The Roman world prized those who contributed to the public good and made a difference. It is critical, if we want to win people to Christ, that we win their respect. The apostle Peter says it best, "Live such good lives among the pagans that, though they accuse you of doing wrong, they may see your good deeds and glorify God on the day he visits us" (1 Pet 2:12). They need to observe the goodness in the Christian—good works in 1 Peter, good hard work here in 1 Thessalonians. Paul uses the same term ("walk") he used in 2:12 and 4:1 to describe the day-by-day conduct of the people of God. Everything we do, including our work ethic, is part of the Christian walk and must exhibit the Spirit's empowering presence. This means we will never allow ourselves to be idle and to lose the respect of those around us.

Those who refuse to work are dependent on others and force them to do what we should be doing for ourselves. This even came to be called the "Protestant work ethic" due to the strong emphasis on this among the Puritans and others. We must be contributing factors in the life of our community. Ephesians 4:28, which I noted above, ends with "doing something useful with their own hands, that they may have something to share with those in need." Note here that the purpose is not to work hard to have more money to spend on ourselves but to work hard so we can help others. This has been completely forgotten in our greedy society. Our task is to enhance the lives of those around us rather than expect them to constantly give to our needs.

———

In this part of the letter we move into the practical material as Paul addresses the moral and ethical issues in this church. He utilizes a covering term that sums up proper Christian conduct—walking so as to please God (vv. 1–2), building on the "worthy of God" concept of 2:12. Every part of our daily conduct falls under the category of that behavior which is acceptable to him. With this he addresses several areas of concern that Timothy communicated to him. Their first concern deals with sexual immorality. As we would expect in a young church, they were struggling with sexual issues, and he makes it all perfectly clear.

Holiness demands purity in this area, and to be separate from the world and set apart for God (the definition of holiness) demands that we gain control of our bodies and refuse to exploit another person by seducing them for our own selfish pleasure (vv. 4–6a). There is a strange myth out there that the saying "What happens in Vegas stays in Vegas" is actually true, and you can get away with what you do "behind closed doors." This is rarely true in an earthly sense, but in terms of divine judgment it is *never* true. Christ is eschatological Judge, and we will pay for our abhorrent behavior. God demands that we remain pure, and to flaunt our sexual freedom is to flaunt our contempt for God himself (vv. 7–8).

The Thessalonian church was also concerned about love, even though they were the archetype of a loving church. They have extended love not just within their own local church but throughout the province, and done so in concrete ways. It is a lesson we need to learn, for showing love takes time and effort, but its rewards are incredible. Like them, we should never be satisfied but seek to show it "more and more" every day (vv. 9–10).

The final issue here (vv. 11–12) is debated but likely stems from a group who stopped working and contributing to society but just sat back waiting for the Lord to return and allowing the rest of the "shallower" Christians who were working to take care of them. They had become selfish busybodies and were turning the community around them against the church due to their selfishness and lack of love. They were losing the respect of the unbelievers and were disrupting the peace and sanctity of the church. Paul urges the saints there to solve the dilemma and turn their whole congregation into trustworthy contributors to those around.

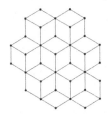

# CONFUSION OVER THE
# FUTURE OF THE DEAD
# AT CHRIST'S RETURN
(4:13–18)

This is now the third issue the Thessalonians had asked Paul about through Timothy—after sexual issues (4:3-8) and the full meaning of brotherly love (4:9-12). This of course is by far the best known, for the passage has spawned enormous debates about the timing of the second coming. They were quite confused about the actual fate of those believers who die before the Lord comes back. Will they have any place in the events initiated by his return? Many Thessalonians were filled with grief at the thought that only the living had a chance to participate in the return of Christ.

There is a great deal of discussion as to why this monumental misunderstanding had taken place among these people. Here are a few of the primary theories:

(1) The most widespread theory says Paul had failed to provide deep instruction about the second coming and the resurrection of the dead (perhaps because he was forced to leave too soon). Yet it is hard to see how he would put off so essential a teaching as this, and he gives no hint of this in this passage. Some even go so far as to say he had not yet worked out his thoughts regarding

those who have died and did not work it all out until he wrote
1 Corinthians 15. This is even more difficult to contemplate; the
issue of the resurrection of the dead is at the heart of Christian
doctrine, and there is no way the apostles and Paul would fail to
understand it for twenty-five years (from Pentecost to the writing
of this epistle). Moreover, he was drawing his basic material from
Jesus (the "word of the Lord" in v. 17), who also had worked it out.

(2) Others think this the result of false teachers, perhaps
**gnostics**, who spiritualized the resurrection and created confusion by saying the resurrection had already happened. But again,
there is no hint of either gnosticism (which came later than this
letter) or any other false doctrine behind this.

(3) Still others think Paul had indeed taught this, but there
was a loss of confidence in this teaching when some key members died. So many had ignored that teaching and gotten confused.
However, the issue was not just about the future of those who have
died but also about the connection of the final resurrection with
the second coming.

(4) In the Old Testament those who are caught up to heaven
(Enoch and Elijah) are always alive, so it is possible that the
Thessalonians took this teaching to mean that the dead would be
in heaven but not have a part in the return of Christ. But the teaching about the resurrection of the dead is too essential a doctrine,
and this is much too speculative. How could recent Gentile converts have even known such a teaching that is clearly Jewish?

(5) The most probable view builds on confusion regarding the
connection between the resurrection from the dead and the return
of Christ applied further to the question of how those who were
deceased would be included in these events. They feared that those
alive would have a huge advantage over those who have died. Paul
responds that if anything, the advantage is the other way; the dead
will rise *first* (v. 16) and then those deceased and those alive will
together "be with the Lord forever" (v. 17).

The one question is why they would grieve so much in this case, but that is no different than our own grief at the death of those we will see again in heaven. We know we will see them again but are still upset over the temporary separation. Our **eschatological** hope is so important a part of our belief system that a single aspect like this can upset us greatly. Paul's purpose is to remove the confusion and to console them with the good news that the dead in Christ will be at no disadvantage at all when Christ returns.

## PAUL WANTS TO INFORM THEM ABOUT THE FUTURE OF THE DECEASED (4:13)

The opening words ("we do not want you to be uninformed") show that this was one of the major questions Timothy brought with him in his report when he returned from his mission to the Thessalonians (3:6). So this is another area in which Paul wants to "supply what is lacking in your faith" (3:10). This was a very serious area of "ignorance," and Paul is undoubtedly shocked at the depth of their misunderstanding. Needless to say, it must be corrected immediately. Paul's frequent use of "brothers and sisters" throughout his letter shows his affection for these people. They are family, and he does not want them to be confused and fearful.

Paul notes that the issue is "about those who sleep in death, so that you do not grieve like the rest of mankind, who have no hope." He uses a common euphemism about death, "sleep," especially apt for the Christian, for whom the earthly death of a believer is actually that, as they know they will "wake up" from their sleep in heaven (see also 1 Cor 7:39; 11:30). It is used also in the Old Testament (Gen 47:30; Job 14:12; Ps 13:3; Dan 12:2), showing a similar belief (though obviously not as well developed) in Israel.

Paul links the grief the Thessalonians felt over these deceased believers with the grief of their pagan neighbors, "who have no hope," who can do nothing but mourn when loved ones die. There is an implied rebuke in this, for the Thessalonians centered on their hope (1:3) and so should not grieve like the pagans. They will grieve, but their mourning will be tempered with the knowledge that a living hope is based on the resurrection of the dead (1 Pet 1:3). The Greco-Roman people had a general belief about crossing the River Styx and walking the Elysian fields forever, but in general death for most meant the end of it all. The philosophers talked about the immortality of the soul, but this was not really held by the general populace. There are many inscriptions regarding the despair common people felt in the face of death. Paul links this despair to the absence of hope, and that is simply not true for the Christian. So the pagan type of grief they felt has no place among Bible-believing Christians.

## PAUL CENTERS ON THE ANCHOR FOR HOPE: CHRISTIAN BELIEF (4:14)

The reason the Christian need not despair is the absolutely certain belief they have about the future. Paul presents this in what is called a first-class condition, with the particle *ei* affirming the truth of the statement ("if" = "since"), so "since we believe that Jesus died and rose again." Paul had already alluded to this promise in 1:10, when he spoke of waiting "for his Son from heaven, whom he raised from the dead." This was an established truth for the early church, anchored in the earliest creed of 1 Corinthians 15:3–5, that "Christ died for our sins ... was buried ... [and] was raised on the third day according to the Scriptures." The purpose of this opening statement is to show them that this core doctrine is at the heart of all Christian belief. So the Christian hope is anchored in absolute truth and in the concrete reality of the resurrection of Jesus.

In the second half of the verse Paul again begins with "so also," effectually turning this into another creedal truth, that "we believe that God will bring with Jesus those who have fallen asleep in him." In 1 Corinthians 15:20, 23, Jesus was raised as the "firstfruits" guaranteeing the future resurrection of the saints. That is the point here as well. When the firstfruits of the harvest appear, the farmer knows the rest are coming. It is an indisputable fact: if Christ was raised, our future resurrection is certain. In fact, to reject our resurrection constitutes a rejection of Jesus' resurrection from the dead and the destruction of all Christian belief (1 Cor 15:12–17). The two are intimately connected throughout the New Testament (Rom 8:11; 1 Cor 15:12–19; 2 Cor 4:14).

Therefore, Paul is saying, since it is certain that Christ was raised from the dead, it is certain that dead believers will be raised with him and accompany him (God "will bring [them] with Jesus") at his return. The implication is that the dead saints are with Jesus in heaven (in keeping with 2 Cor 5:1–10) and are brought not from the grave (the error of soul sleep[1]) but from heaven. In this case death is truly sleep, and the moment the soul is transported from heaven (at death) they "wake up" and look into the face of the risen Lord. By saying this Paul clears up any confusion that the dead are at a disadvantage with respect to the **parousia**. If anything, they have the advantage, for they will come with Christ to meet those who are still alive. Christ is both the agent in whom we die ("fallen asleep through [*dia*] him") and the one who makes our resurrection possible ("bring with Jesus").

## PAUL TURNS TO THE TEACHING OF JESUS (4:15–17)

### THE FATE OF THOSE WHO ARE ALIVE (4:15)

This verse begins with "according to the Lord's word," but there is no recorded saying of Jesus that matches the material in these three verses. Some have said this stems from a Christian prophet who spoke in the name of the risen Lord. This is very doubtful, for

---

1. This view holds that from the moment of death until the resurrection, the deceased are in an unconscious state awaiting the parousia (return of Christ). As we will see in Phil 1:20–23 and 2 Cor 5:8, the truth is an "intermediate state" in which the soul is conscious and with the Lord in heaven awaiting the glorified body, which will be given at the second coming.

there is no evidence that such would ever be seen as the words of Jesus himself, and the phrase "word of the Lord" is never used of prophecy in the New Testament.

This could be a saying not recorded anywhere else, but it is more likely Paul is giving us a paraphrase of Jesus' teaching rather than quoting an exact saying. He does this elsewhere (1 Cor 7:10, 25; 9:14; 11:23–25), and the content of this material comes close to Matthew 24:29–31 (see also 1 Cor 15:51–52). In this passage, most agree that verse 15 is Paul's summary of the material with verses 16–17 constituting the saying of Jesus itself.

The message the Thessalonians need to hear is: "we who are still alive, who are left until the coming of the Lord, will certainly not precede those who have fallen asleep." The "we" both includes Paul with his readers and provides a separation of "we who are alive" from those who have died. It seems clear from this that the issue had to do with the relation of the deceased saints to the living saints at the return of Christ, probably meaning they thought the dead would lose out on ascending to heaven at that time. Paul thought the event would be soon and that he would still be alive when it happened, and he wanted to remove that mistaken fear on their part.

His primary emphasis is that those still alive will not "precede" those who are deceased to meet the Lord or to go to heaven. He already made this clear in verse 14, when he said Jesus would "bring with him" those who have died. In other words, they were already in heaven and would actually come with Jesus. In verse 16 Paul gives the other side: "the dead in Christ will rise first," a reference as we will see to their resurrection bodies. In other words, their soul is with the Lord, and their bodies will arise near the time those who are alive are taken up. The two groups will probably receive their heavenly bodies together. So it is doubly true that the living will not precede the dead at the parousia. Both will have their place in the glorious event of Christ's second coming, and there is no advantage either way.

THE PLACE OF THE DEAD AT THE SECOND COMING (4:16)

Paul now proceeds to cite in his own words what Jesus had taught. It is difficult to know whether he is using Matthew 24 or his general knowledge of the Olivet Discourse that Matthew also used. Interestingly, this is the most complete list of the three (Matt 24:29-31; 1 Cor 15:51-52). Given the **apocalyptic** language and the remarkable symbolism, real questions exist regarding how literal or metaphorical the details are meant to be.

I grew up (many of you readers likely have as well) with what is called "the newspaper approach," taking all end-times details as exactly literal and forming a timeline for the future. Yet after writing a book on hermeneutics (how to interpret the Bible) and a commentary on the book of Revelation, I have come to realize it is not easy, for we have to decide what is literal and what is symbolic. For instance, will there be an actual angelic voice or blast of a trumpet, or are they metaphors that represent the coming of Christ from heaven to earth (an event that is definitely literal)? With this in mind, let's look at the details one at a time:

1. "The Lord himself will come down from heaven": This is the language of "parousia" (Greek for the "coming" of the Lord), a term used for the pomp and circumstance of an imperial visit to a city and the celebration it always caused. At the occasion, the city officials and a large group of the people would come out and meet the ruler with joy. This is the ultimate parousia, as the "Lord himself," the King of kings, comes for his people.

2. "With a loud command": It could be that this is the primary event, with both the angel's voice and the trumpet describing further the shouted command. But Paul seems to present them as separate details, and I will treat them as such. The term for "command," *keleusma*, refers to a military order shouted to the soldiers or an official governmental order. The military command is the more likely here. The descending Christ is the likely commander giving the

order, as in John 5:25 ("the dead will hear the voice of the Son of God and those who hear will live"), 28–29 ("all who are in their graves will hear his voice and come out").

3. "With the voice of an archangel": There is not much on archangels in Scripture—here and Jude 9 (the archangel Michael). They seem to be ruling angels of the angelic realm. Seven are named in 1 Enoch 20:1–7 (Uriel, Raphael, Raguel, Michael, Saraqa'el, Gabriel, Remiel). Angels are often connected to the day of the Lord (Matt 13:39; 24:31; 25:31; 1 Cor 6:3; 2 Thess 1:7; Jude 14). The "voice" probably designates the involvement of the angelic armies in these final events.

4. "With the trumpet call of God": Trumpets were used in most aspects of ancient life to designate military activity, athletic events, worship and sacrifices, and the movements of the king. Most important for this is the use of trumpets to herald imperial edicts and major announcements. Its presence at the day of the Lord is noted in Isaiah 27:13; Joel 2:1; Zephaniah 1:14–16; Zechariah 9:14. It is a marker of the end-time events in Matthew 24:31; 1 Corinthians 15:52; and often in Revelation (8:2, 6, 13; 9:14; 11:15). Here it may signal the moment when the dead come to life.

5. "The dead in Christ will rise first": Only the dead saints are raised at this time. The unsaved, so far as I see in Scripture, are not raised until the final judgment (Rev 20:13). Two critical aspects must be understood. First, their souls are already with God, as we noted above, so these are the resurrection bodies that are combined with their soul/spirit "in the air" (v. 17). Second, this takes place before the living saints are caught up in what has come to be called "the rapture." There is no disadvantage whatsoever for the dead; in fact, with their being *first*, the advantage if anything is all theirs. They are the preeminent ones (of course, in reality all are equal in Christ).

## THE PLACE OF THE LIVING WITH THE DEAD AT THE SECOND COMING (4:17)

There are three acts in the drama here. In act 1 Christ returns, and with him are the souls of the deceased saints who have been with him in heaven (in the intermediate state). Act 2 takes place when they arrive in the heavens/sky of this world, and the living saints are caught up to the Lord. Now in act 3 the two, the dead and the living, are first of all united with each other ("caught up together") and then with their glorified bodies as both groups (now one) join the Lord "in the air."

The first part of this verse describes the "rapture," when "we who are still alive and are left will be caught up together with them in the clouds to meet the Lord in the air." This provides the final piece of the puzzle for the Thessalonians. To be "caught up together" is to be "snatched" or "seized" from this earthly environment by God. It is not a violent metaphor, but it is a strong image of being taken up by God. The living will have no advantage, nor will there be any favoritism. The two—the dead and the living—will in the end be reunited with absolutely no disparity between the two groups. For us the message is critical—the future of God's people is beyond belief. Whether alive or dead when Christ comes, we will receive an eternal, perfect, glorified body, which will never again know illness or deprivation of any kind, and become the heavenly people of God (Phil 3:20-21).

When the two groups become one they rise together "in the clouds." Clouds were Old Testament symbols of theophany (a manifestation of God), symbolizing the **Shekinah** (God dwelling among his people) glory of God in Exodus 13:21; 16:10; 19:16. Clouds also stemmed from the dust clouds of war chariots and became the imperial chariot for God (Ps 18:10; Isa 19:1). In the New Testament on the Mount of Transfiguration, the cloud that encompassed Jesus and the disciples was this Shekinah cloud of glory (Matt 17:5; Mark 9:7; Luke 9:34). This is also the significance of clouds in apocalyptic passages, as Jesus ascended to heaven in a cloud (Acts 1:9) and here and in Matthew 24:30 will come back in a cloud, building on Daniel 7:13 ("one like a son of man, coming with the clouds of heaven").

The clouds carry them "to meet the Lord in the air." The "meeting" (*eis apantēsin*) pictures a delegation exiting the city to meet a visiting official and escort him with honor into the city. The picture is of the King of kings meeting his entourage with great pomp and circumstance in order to bestow high honor on them. They meet "in the air," which is more than just the sky as we know it but that place between God's heaven and earth where God and the angels function. It was often considered the home of demonic spirits, but here it is the home of the angelic realm.

There may be a hint of the defeat of the demonic forces, but that would only be implicit, as Paul's emphasis is on the glorious reunion of both the dead and the living with the Lord. A similar implicit teaching might also be the future descent of the victorious Lord with his people back to earth. In Revelation 17:14, 19:14, the saints join Christ's heavenly army and proceed with him to defeat the antichrist and the forces of evil.

Paul omits the events that take place between the parousia (Rev 19) and eternity in heaven (Rev 21)—the tribulation period, the defeat of the antichrist, the millennium, and the great white throne judgment (Rev 19–20)—probably because he didn't need to tell everything in order to comfort the readers. He closes with, "And so we will be with the Lord forever," our eternal home with the angels and the Godhead in heaven. This is the end product and goal of all the events described in verses 13–18. The citation of Jesus' teaching ended at our meeting the Lord in the air, and this concluding comment is Paul's own joyous exclamation. It is interesting that he doesn't say where that eternal home will be. Yet it is implicit. The Lord descended from heaven (v. 16a), and it is probably meant to be assumed that he would take his resurrected saints back to heaven with him.

## THE PURPOSE IN ALL THIS IS
## ENCOURAGEMENT (4:18)

Paul has already provided the perfect culmination for these incredible truths. Not only is there no need to be discouraged and grieving over a mistaken view of the place of those deceased at the return of Christ, but there is also every reason to be filled with joy at the final eternal destiny in heaven. So he concludes with the purpose of this section and a mission for these readers to the rest of the Thessalonian church: "Therefore encourage one another with these words."

He has used *parakaleō* often in this letter (2:12; 3:2, 7; 4:1, 10, 18; 5:11, 14). While at times it refers to exhortation, here he uses it for comfort or encouragement (see also 3:2, 7; 5:11). Paul has cleared up their sad misunderstanding, and what he has shared in verses 15–17 can only result in exultation. The rest of the church needs to be comforted and to have their fears assuaged. Their former grief at the death of their loved ones, feeling that they may miss out on the return of Christ, can be completely reversed. The truth about the future of saints who die is reunion, not loss. Not only will they have a part in the second coming, but they will also have a central role and be united with those who are still alive, receive glorified bodies, and spend eternity together in heaven. It don't get much better than that!

Moreover, Paul gives them a mission, commissioning them to take the good news to others and comfort the rest of the church. It is time to be eschatological evangelists, to comfort and galvanize one another with this incredible truth. Good news is meant to be spread. When we receive a great gift, say we win a prize or get an unexpected check in the mail, we call everyone we know and share the news of the bounty with them. The news he shared was infinitely better than a monetary gift, for it is eternal in scope. I picture the Thessalonians running from house to house sharing these great "words."

## EXCURSUS: THE HISTORY OF THE PRE-TRIBULATION RAPTURE

This passage has become a focal point of a vociferous debate in the church over the timing of the second coming and the catching up of the saints to heaven. The particular form of the debate we see in our time all began with the Plymouth Brethren movement in England in the 1830s, when a new teaching arose that came to be called "dispensationalism." According to this teaching, biblical history can be divided into a series of epochs or "dispensations" in which God works in certain ways to bring sinful humankind back to himself.

The key for the issue of the second coming is the contrast in dispensationalism between the old- and new-covenant periods. God centered on Israel as his people and expected them to follow Jesus. When they rejected Jesus, however, he turned to a new dispensation, a parenthesis in his plan called the church age. This will continue until Christ returns, and then he will bring the Jewish people back to himself (his original intention) in a national revival that will occur after a "secret rapture" in which the church will be taken up to heaven and the new Jewish converts will remain on earth for the seven-year "tribulation period." At the end of that seven years, they too will be caught up when Christ comes to destroy the antichrist and the forces of evil.

This came to be called the "pre-tribulation rapture" of the saints because it came at the beginning of that final period of history, when the antichrist will seek to wipe out the people of God (Rev 7:14; 13:14–17). This passage is a main pillar for that position, with its detailed picture of the "rapture" and especially the command to "comfort" people with this truth. The argument is that there would not be much comfort if it meant we had to pass through the terrible events of the tribulation period.

I cannot discuss this in depth, as entire books are devoted to this issue. All I can do is briefly share my perspective. I grew up "pre-trib," but when I started studying it in depth I found myself rethinking my position. I came to conclude that Paul would not recognize the dispensational interpretation of this passage because (1) the "comfort" here is not escaping persecution but rather the knowledge that we will all share equally in this eternal reward. Moreover, (2) the New Testament makes it a privilege, not a horror, to share "participation in his sufferings" (Eph 3:10). So Paul would never accept this argument. Further, (3) there is no basis for a "secret rapture" here or in other passages. Every detail is public; when Christ returns, the entire world will know it.

My problem too is that I don't see in the New Testament two returns of Christ seven years apart but rather one return, and that is more likely at the end of a tribulation period (called the "post-tribulation" return). Christ will come with the dead, catch the living up to himself, give them their glorified bodies, and they will then join the heavenly army (Rev 17:14, 19:14) and proceed down to destroy the forces of evil. However, I have colleagues, family, and friends on the other side, and we must learn to "agree to disagree" on these issues. Revelation 3:10 is an important passage for the pre-trib position if it means that "keep you from the hour of trial" means to remove you before the tribulation period begins. (Post-tribbers think it means God will protect you during that period.) Both are viable and possible, and all any of us can do is prayerfully consider the data and make up our minds. This is not an issue on which we should go to war against each other, as has too often taken place.

———

This passage is at the heart of the Christian faith, for it tells us what awaits us at the end of human history. For the Christian life does not end at death, but in reality it actually begins at death, when our temporary, frail, earthly bodies are replaced by heavenly bodies that will live for eternity. The Thessalonians precipitated the confusion by their mistaken belief that those who die in the Lord will miss the return of Christ, when only the living will be caught up to him. So Paul tells us the truth about the parousia, that the dead will not only have a part to play but will actually accompany the Lord from heaven and will meet those living saints in the air. Far from missing the event, they will have "first" place in it.

The events and persons involved in this are extremely "comforting" to all true Christians. We (whether alive or dead) will be the central focus of all these events, and incredible imagery will attend them. The angelic realm will have a part, and the truth is that after we receive our resurrection bodies we will join the angels as part of heaven's armies and then take part in the destruction of the forces of evil. We will join Jesus on the "clouds" of his war chariot as he arrives and then proceeds to earth in victory. We, the living and the dead, will have joined together "in the air" as we proceed to our new bodies and to join as one with the returning Christ to share his glory and his victory.

With all of this it is foolish to fight over an issue like the timing of this event vis-à-vis the tribulation period (pre- vs. mid- vs. post-tribulation events). There are no unambiguous statements and so no way to adjudicate absolutely between the positions. God never considered it important enough to make completely clear, so we should center on the true "comfort" of this passage and not get caught up in internecine debates over timing.

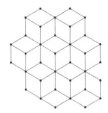

# GETTING READY FOR THE
# DAY OF THE LORD
(5:1–11)

There are two major events connected to the eschaton, or end of
this world—the return of Christ, centering on the catching up
of the saints; and the day of the Lord, centering on the judgment
and destruction of evil. Paul covered the first in 4:13–18, and now
the second in 5:1–11. In both the question is the involvement of the
saints in the event. It is more difficult to know why Paul addresses
this and what if anything was the anxiety of the Thessalonians
on this issue. While in 4:13–18 Paul addressed the fate of deceased
believers, this passage probably concerns the fate of the saints
who are still alive when this event takes place. So it may be that
they were worried whether they would escape these judgments.

The Thessalonians were very interested in the day of the Lord
and the judgment of those who had so severely opposed and persecuted them. They needed to know that their future vindication
was a sure thing and that they themselves would be part of the
victors rather than suffer with the vanquished. Paul answers this
in verses 1–3. At the same time, they themselves were unprepared,
and Paul had to challenge them to be ready. Still, unlike for the
pagans that day will not come like a "thief in the night" for believers, for they are "children of the day" (v. 5) and are not appointed

to wrath but salvation (v. 9). Here too they can be encouraged regarding their part in the future of God's people.

## PAUL TEACHES THE SUDDEN DESTRUCTION AT THE DAY OF THE LORD (5:1–3)

### ITS UNEXPECTED NATURE (5:1–2)

Paul begins this passage with "now about" (*peri de*), which as we saw in 4:9, 13, introduces a new topic for discussion. The little particle *de* has been at the heart of the pre-trib/post-trib debate over whether the rapture passage and the day of the Lord passage describe two separate events (separated by seven years, so the pre-trib argument goes) or two aspects of the same event (so the post-trib argument). I would conclude the answer is a both-and. The day of the Lord is a new topic asked through Timothy, but the return of Christ in New Testament **eschatology** brought about the day of the Lord. The **parousia** in Revelation 19:11–16 leads immediately to the defeat of the antichrist/beast (19:17–21) and then to the millennium and final judgment (20:11–15). They are interdependent aspects of a single event, the eschaton (the Greek word for "end").

Paul's purpose here is to address the "times and dates [seasons]." The two terms (*chronos* and *kairos*) are virtual synonyms and together make a kind of set formula that refers to the timing of the events that will bring this world to a close and initiate eternity (Dan 2:21; Acts 1:7). This was a very popular issue in both testaments, and both Israel and the church were highly interested in the "times" during which God was going to end this evil world (Jer 6:15; 10:15; 27:4, 31; Dan 8:17; 12:6; Matt 24:3; Mark 8:32–33; 1 Cor 4:5). In Peter's opinion, this question dominated the prophetic period (1 Pet 1:10–11).

Paul tells them, "about times and dates we do not need to write to you." This goes back to 4:2, where he had told them, "you know what instructions we gave you" (see also 1:8, 4:9). Paul had taught them well about these issues, and there was actually nothing new to say. Probably they wanted to know exactly when Christ was returning and what they could do about it (don't we all!). He reminds them here that they already have all they are going to get, and it is more than sufficient. Probably, the rest of this passage (vv. 2–11) is material he had told them before and wants them to recall. The basic point is that they cannot know any more about the timing of the end and simply must be ready at all times. I will explore this further in verses 4–8.

In verse 2 he explicitly states why he doesn't need to write about this: "For [*gar*, telling the reason why] you know very well that the day of the Lord will come like a thief in the night." He has used "know" in every chapter to stress the knowledge they already have on an issue (1:4, 5; 2:1, 2, 5, 11; 3:3, 4; 4:2). Here he makes it emphatic by adding *akribōs*, "accurately, certainly" (NIV "very well") to show they have all the knowledge they will ever need, in fact, all the knowledge that Paul himself has. There is a play on words on this—they know very well that they know almost nothing about the "times and seasons."

What they know is that "the day of the Lord" is coming "like a thief in the night." The day of the Lord is a technical phrase in the Old Testament for the eschaton, that end-of-the-world event when God comes to judge the world, destroy evil, and vindicate his people (among others, Isa 13:6–13; Ezek 30:2–3; Joel 1:15; 2:1; Zech 14; Mal 4:5). Paul uses it often (1 Cor 5:5; 2 Thess 2:2), at times changing it to "the day of the Lord Jesus" (1 Cor 1:8; 2 Cor 1:4; Phil 1:6, 10), usually with the full imagery from the Old Testament. Judgment and destruction are the primary word pictures associated with it (2 Thess 1:6–10).

The imagery of coming "like a thief in the night" always occurs in passages about the judgment of the unbelievers. It stems from the teaching of Jesus (Matt 24:43; Luke 12:39) and then was used in the letters (2 Pet 3:10; Rev 3:3, 16:5) to stress both the unexpected nature and the swiftness of the second coming of Christ. In the same way that a thief seeks to surprise and fool

the householder, so Christ will choose a moment no one can pre-
dict. This states clearly that there is no use trying to compute the
time of Christ's coming. God does not want it to be known. For
us it means that so-called prophecy preachers in our day should
stop their attempts to figure out the time of the second coming.
First, none of them have ever been right; second, it is wrong for
them even to try.

## Its Mode: Sudden Destruction (5:3)

The parousia Paul mentioned in 4:13–18 is for the believer and
means joy and life. The day of the Lord here is for the unbeliever
and means horror and destruction. You cannot read this without feeling the sinister, menacing overtones: "While people are
saying, 'Peace and safety [or "security"],' destruction will come
on them suddenly." "Peace and security" stems from the Roman
propaganda machine with its false *Pax Romana* ("Roman peace")
motto. This was a completely fake promise, for that "peace" was
accomplished only by the Roman sword and military power. This
is not Paul's normal language but is cited from Roman slogans.

The Old Testament prophets often spoke of false prophets who
promised peace but never delivered (Jer 6:14; 8:11, "'Peace, peace,'
they say, when there is no peace"; also Ezek 13:10–16; Mic 3:5). This
is the case here and in our time. Politicians (have they ever been
so bad as they are now?) will always promise, often without even
caring whether they can deliver on the promise. This is exactly
how Satan (John 8:44, "the father of lies") operates. The world
thinks it is safe and secure, but that is bravado, and the wake-up
call will be terrible indeed. Since Thessalonica was not only pro-
Roman but also a near copy of Rome, these promises were very
important to her populace. But her security was a facade and very
temporary in nature, as we will see.

At that moment of false peace, Paul relates, "destruction
will come on them suddenly," as we saw in verse 2 above. The
term for "destruction," *olethros*, only occurs in 1 Corinthians 5:5;

2 Thessalonians 1:9; 1 Timothy 6:9, and elsewhere, always picturing God's final judgment of the wicked. It pictures both the annihilation of the wicked and their eternal separation from God.

He adds further imagery, describing the coming of final judgment "as labor pains on a pregnant woman." This image is frequent in Scripture (Isa 13:6-8, 21:3; Jer 22:23; Hos 13:13; Mic 4:9-10) for both the intense pain and the suddenness as well as unexpectedness of the onslaught. The point is that those who put their trust in the world (Rome) have absolutely no hope and will be prey for the certain judgment that is coming on those who live for this life rather than for God. The added "and they will not escape" makes this totally clear. There is no escape whatsoever for those who deliberately choose sin (Rom 1:18-32) and ignore God.

## PAUL CONTRASTS THE BELIEVER (LIGHT) WITH THE UNBELIEVER (DARKNESS) (5:4-8)

### BELIEVERS AS THE CHILDREN OF LIGHT (5:4-5)

Paul now shifts his focus from the unsaved (v. 3) back to the Thessalonian Christians and tells them why they can have "peace and safety" regarding the day of the Lord. To the unsaved, it is sudden, and they are completely unprepared. The saved are ready, prepared by their **apocalyptic** expectations. They don't know *when* it will come but are ready when it does arrive. The reason they need not fear is because "you, brothers and sisters, are not in darkness so that this day should surprise you like a thief." There are actually two reasons here: (1) as "brothers and sisters" they are part of the family of God and so will be vindicated, not punished, on that day; (2) they are not in the "darkness" of sin like the unbelievers but belong to the "day" of salvation.

The term *adelphoi* ("brothers") occurs fourteen times in 1 Thessalonians and is part of Paul's comprehensive use of family imagery in this letter—infants in 2:7a, nursing mothers in 2:7b, fathers in 2:11, and siblings throughout the letter. He wants them to know how precious they are to their heavenly Father and how little they have to fear as a result.

"Darkness" refers to the world of sin that is completely devoid of the light of God (John 3:19–21; 2 Cor 6:14; Eph 5:11; 6:12). The light-darkness motif is well-known in Scripture (Prov 4:18–19; Isa 59:9–10; John 1:5; 1 John 2:8–9). To be in darkness is to be blind to the light of God and to have no hope. It connotes both the state of sin and the presence of ignorance. In their sin, the people of darkness do not even want to know the truth.

On the other hand, these people of light embrace and treasure truth, so "this day should [not] surprise you like a thief." So long as they remain faithful and live as children of the day they will be ready and need not fear but rather can look forward to the day of the Lord, for it will be a day of victory and reward for them. Far from being a surprise, it will be a relief, for their struggle will be over forever.

In verse 5 Paul takes the imagery further and adds detail, telling them, "You are all children of the light and children of the day." This is quite emphatic—Paul includes every single believer. On this there is no distinction between mature Christians and young Christians. All belong to the light. To be a "child of" something is to belong to it and be characterized by it. So these people belong to the day and are characterized by the light of God. If darkness is the sinful condition and ignorance, then light stands for knowledge (a constant emphasis in this letter) and salvation. The idea of "children of the day" adds an eschatological nuance. They are no longer of this world but belong to the new "day" that is coming. Christ inaugurated this new era at his first coming, and it is gradually coming to fruition, soon to culminate in his second coming.

The contrast continues in the second half of the verse: "We do not belong to the night or to the darkness." There is a **chiastic** organization for emphasis:

> A You are all children of the light
> > B and children of the day.
> > B′ We do not belong to the night
> A′ or to the darkness.

There is no new message. Rather, this says the same thing negatively. Still, it gives great stress to the important point here. We are no longer citizens of this world, to be characterized by the things of this world. That is no longer us. The Thessalonians have nothing to worry about on judgment day, for they no longer belong to night or darkness.

## CONCLUSION: A NEW LIFESTYLE (5:6–8)

The contrast between night and day has been established. Now Paul develops the ethical consequences.

### Holy people are not like others (5:6)

I have noted several times that holiness means to be set apart, to separate ourselves from the world and be set apart for God. Therefore Paul says, "let us not be like others, who are asleep." Since they belong to the night, they sleep through the day. The children of light, on the other hand, are called to be "awake and sober." He chooses a somewhat unusual verb for "sleep" here, *katheudō*, which speaks of those who are unaware and apathetic of the moral implications of what they are doing. They sleep and head for destruction and virtually don't care about the direction they are heading.

We have an English phrase, "hoi polloi," that refers to the general public. It is borrowed from the Greek, and Paul uses it here in "let us not be like others" (Greek, "like the rest"), similar to 4:13, "so that you do not grieve like the rest of mankind." "The rest" are clearly the rest of sinful humankind, who have rejected Christ and have no hope. They not only know nothing about the way to salvation and life; they don't want to know anything and prefer their indifferent, deadly pattern of conduct. This is not the case for the children of God, a situation for which we all should be eternally grateful.

As a result, they reject the apathetic slumber of the unsaved and want to remain "awake and sober." "Awake" means much more than the conscious state and connotes an alert, vigilant readiness to act. Paul is speaking of a readiness or preparedness for Christ's return. The term (*gregoreō*) means to be awake and watchful and is often used of a guard on a city's wall, prepared for whatever happens. It is frequent in Matthew 24–25 in the midst of the parables dealing with being ready for the Lord's return ("keep watch, because you do not know on what day your Lord will come," Matt 24:42). These parables (the wise servant, the ten virgins, the talents) all warn Jesus' disciples of the terrible consequences of spiritual indifference.

The second verb (*nēphō*) means "sober" in the sense of self-controlled, in command of yourself. It occurs especially in eschatological passages referring to those who control their conduct with respect to the end times, thus being ready for the Lord's return (1 Thess 5:8; 2 Tim 4:5; 1 Pet 4:7; 5:8). The saints cannot be merely passive, waiting for Christ's return. They are commanded to be conducting themselves appropriately, as in the conclusion to the lengthy discussion of the final resurrection in 1 Corinthians 15, "Therefore ... stand firm. Let nothing move you. Always give yourselves fully to the work of the Lord" (1 Cor 15:58).

### The unbeliever's deeds of darkness (5:7)

The domain of the non-Christian is darkness, and their deeds are nighttime activities, namely, sleep and drunkenness. The allusion to drunken behavior seems strange here until we realize it is due to a play on words, establishing two contrasts with verse 6. The believer is awake while the unbeliever is asleep, and the believer is sober while the unbeliever is drunk. This is so because the domain of the believer is the day, while the unbeliever belongs to the night. This means that God's people are prepared and ready, while the people of the world are indifferent and will be spiritually asleep when Christ comes. In the first-century world it was disgraceful to get drunk during the day; all heavy drinking took place at night.

Drunkenness is a euphemism here for those who live for pleasure and excess rather than for God. The world is actually quite disciplined, but their self-control is entirely in the area of self-centered, hedonistic conduct. They live for their pleasures, their greed, in general for the things of the world rather than for the things of God.

### The armor of the Christian (5:8)

After the build-up, the conclusion here is quite easy to draw. "Since we belong to the day" we can have nothing to do with the deeds of those who belong to the night. The we/they contrast is very stark. "They" belong to the night and are asleep with respect to the things of God, "but we" are of the day and so must "be sober," seeking the self-control of verse 6. As people of light, our lives must be characterized by the light of God, which means disciplined conduct in light of the soon return of Christ.

The second half of the verse moves us into military imagery, another common feature of eschatological contexts drawn from the army-of-God language of the Old Testament, for instance, "the Lord of hosts" as "the Lord of heaven's armies," looking to the angelic realm as the military arm of God. The use of armor-of-God imagery is drawn from Isaiah 59:17, "He put on righteousness as his breastplate, and the helmet of salvation on his head." The light-darkness imagery of this section reminds Paul of another fact, that the people of darkness are under the power of demonic forces, as in Ephesians 6:10–12: "Put on the full armor of God ... for our struggle is ... against the powers of this dark world." This is spiritual warfare, and God's people need God's armor for the battle.

This tells us how we gain control of ourselves: "let us be sober, *putting on* faith and love as a breastplate." The imagery for Paul's readers is obvious, as Roman soldiers were everywhere, and in a pro-Roman city like Thessalonica they would be lauded. In many writings of the first century, armor was a natural metaphor for ethical and moral principles, so this was readily understandable. Interestingly, in Isaiah it is God the Divine Warrior who clothes himself with this armor, while here it is God's people who do so. The picture is the warrior King leading his children to become warrior princes and princesses in the heavenly army.

Paul uses military imagery often (Rom 13:12; 2 Cor 6:7; 10:3–5; Eph 6:14–17; Phil 2:25; 2 Tim 2:3–4), always to show that we are in what could be called a "holy war" against spiritual forces. He adapts the Isaiah 59 imagery to highlight the spiritual triad of 1:3, faith, love, and hope. Isaiah's "righteousness as his breastplate" is changed to "faith and love as a breastplate," and the "helmet of salvation" is now "the hope of salvation as a helmet." As I pointed out at 1:3, Paul often uses this list as the center of the believer's arsenal of weapons against sin and evil. When God's people put these three into practice, spiritual victory follows.

To "put on" or "clothe yourself with" a virtue is to make it the key quality defining your conduct. They must be characterized in their relationships and the way they live their life with faith, love, and hope. The breastplate and helmet were defensive pieces of armor, meant to protect the soldier from harm in the midst of battle. So here these virtues protect the believer from "the flaming arrows of the evil one" (Eph 6:16) and from temptation. The Thessalonians were indeed victorious in these very areas (2 Thess 1:3–4) and were well prepared for the return of Christ ("the hope of salvation"). Their faith in God and love for the saints (1:7–8) were well known everywhere, and that led to the hope for the future. The "hope of salvation," many think, is the main point here and refers to the absolute certainty that their future salvation at the second coming is guaranteed by God.

## THE DESTINY OF THE BELIEVER IS
## SALVATION AND LIFE (5:9-10)

Now Paul explains why (*hoti*, "because, for") the Christian lives in "the hope of salvation." There is no need for any believer to fear the coming eschaton (end of the world), which apparently was the case with some of the Thessalonians. Paul responds to this with another contrast, this time concerning the destiny of the saved versus the unsaved: "God did not appoint us to suffer wrath but to receive salvation through our Lord Jesus Christ."

The verb *tithēmi* is another term for divine election: God has "chosen" or "destined" us not to suffer his wrath but to receive his salvation. The language connotes more than predestination to salvation but especially God's choosing us as his special people to live for him according to his will. So "salvation" here is a covering term for the Christian life as a whole, sanctification as well as justification. We are saved by the blood of Christ, sanctified by the Holy Spirit, and then enter our final eternal salvation. This includes all, with a special emphasis on final salvation at the return of Christ.

We were "destined" to suffer trials and persecution (3:3) but not to suffer the wrath of God. The people of darkness are also the people of wrath. Paul promised the saints in 1:10 that Jesus will rescue them "from the coming wrath," that eternal punishment to which the sinners will be assigned at the last judgment. The time when that will take place is "the day of the Lord" in 5:2, defined as sudden destruction in 5:3. Paul's purpose is to allay the fears of these people and help them to realize that they will have no part in it whatsoever, for God has destined or elected them not to wrath but to salvation.

The primary function of this, however, is on the positive side, obtaining salvation through the Lord. The emphasis of *peripoiēsis* is on the active "obtaining" more than the passive "possessing," but that does not mean that we gain it by our own efforts. Rather, it is our faith-decision to accept God's gift of salvation. This is shown in the added "through our Lord Jesus Christ," stressing Christ as the instrument (*dia*, "through") of our salvation. Christ purchased our salvation by his atoning sacrifice, so that his blood led to the forgiveness of our sins. As we turn to him in faith, God declares us to be right with him and destines us for final salvation.

Paul stated the task of Christ in making salvation possible in verse 9 and now explicitly in verse 10, exploring the death/life antithesis. We obtain salvation only because "he died for us." The important phrase is "for us," with *hyper* marking his substitutionary death "on our behalf" (see Mark 10:45 [with *anti*]; 1 Cor 15:3). We were on the cross with Christ, and our sins were covered by his blood. God saw his redemptive work, attributed it to our account, and declared us innocent. Through this we were delivered from his wrath and destined for eternal salvation in heaven.

The result (*hina*, "so that") is that "whether we are awake or asleep, we may live together with him." If we understood this in the way of verses 6–7, those "awake" would be spiritually vigilant, mature believers, and those "asleep" would be lazy, indifferent unbelievers. However, the image here goes back to 4:13–18, where those awake are the saints still alive and those asleep are the deceased believers. There we learned that when Christ returns, the two groups will be reunited, so here we see the results of that truth as all believers "live together with him" in heaven.

## COMFORT AND BUILD UP ONE ANOTHER (5:11)

After Paul's discussion in 4:13–17 of the future reunion of deceased saints with those who are still alive at the return of Christ, he concluded, "Therefore encourage one another with these words." Now after his presentation in 5:1–10 of the glorious future of all the saints when the day of the Lord arrives, he concludes with the same words and adds a further command, "and build each other up." How could we not be tremendously encouraged to learn that (1) we belong to the day (v. 5), (2) we can clothe ourselves with the armor of God (v. 8), and (3) God has destined us for eternal salvation (v. 9).

Armed with these incredible theological truths, we are not only comforted but also galvanized to action. The term for the Christian "build up" is *oikodomeō*, an architectural metaphor used for the construction of Rome's "world wonder" buildings like the Colosseum or the temple of Diana. In the Old Testament, God built Israel, his people (Ps 28:5; Jer 24:6; 42:10), and the early church borrowed this imagery to describe God's work in the church (Rom 14:29; Eph 4:12, 16, 29). The point here is the same as elsewhere.

The saints need to join God and build each other up. We are all responsible to "build each other up." This is a very important point for the church today. None of us can overcome the flesh and attain spiritual victory on our own. We need each other. This is a special phrase for "each other," *eis ton hena*. It is not just a synonym for "one another" but adds meaning, an "each one of you" aspect that emphasizes a one-on-one environment in the church. The stress is on every single one of us involved with each other. I need you, and you need me. We will both grow where I help you in your areas of weakness, and you do the same with me.

Paul concludes by acknowledging, "just as in fact you are doing." I pray all our churches would be able to hear that from Paul. This is a very positive letter, the polar opposite to the Corinthian letters. This is the third time he has said such a thing (see 4:1, 10). They dare not be satisfied with their current state (as encouraging as it is) but need to keep working hard at their Christian walk. There are still things "lacking" in their Christian life (3:10), and we never stop growing. The great thing about the Christian life is that the adventure never stops!

———

Paul covers two critical aspects of the doctrine of last things (eschatology) in this passage, and the perspective of both is the place that the saints have in these final events. The first was the part they would play in the return of Christ itself, the subject of 4:13–18. The second is the part they will play in contrast to unbelievers at the day of the Lord (the last judgment), the subject of 5:1–11. The first emphasis is the unexpected nature of its coming (vv. 2–3). The one thing we know is how little we know about its coming, for it will arrive "like a thief in the night," suddenly and when we least expect it. When it comes, it will bring total destruction in its wake. It is right to be filled with fright!

Believers, on the other hand, need not fear, for that day will not be unexpected; our apocalyptic perspective and the God-centered life it produces will make us ready, for we are people of the day, not the night. And we dwell in the domain of light rather than darkness (vv. 4–5). For us it will mean vindication and victory. We have the "peace and safety" they do not.

Verses 6–8 are very critical for us today, for being "awake and sober" calls for a highly active, rigidly disciplined life of service to the Lord and a lifestyle dedicated to pleasing him. Too often I find Christians living a complacent, passive life of attending church regularly and trying to do good works. That is all well and good but not what Paul has in mind. For these dynamic Christians God's armor in Isaiah 59:17 becomes their armor, and rather than being passive toward sin they go to war against all evil, putting into practice the faith, love, and hope that characterize them as they battle against wickedness in this world.

The saints need not worry about the day of the Lord. Quite the opposite! They long for it, for God has destined them for salvation, not wrath (vv. 9–10). To them, God is first Abba and only then Judge. For them that day will culminate their lives with joy, and eternal bliss will be theirs forever. For the sinner, it will be a time of unmitigated terror as they discover the utter folly of all their plans without God. The saints, who in their plans centered on God and on pleasing him, will experience the final stage of "living together with him" in oneness with the Godhead and with all the other saints, who will enjoy eternity as one loving family.

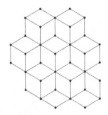

# FINAL INSTRUCTIONS
# AND LETTER CLOSING
(5:12–28)

P aul has dealt with the major issues (sexual conduct, brotherly love, **eschatological** confusion) in 4:1–5:11, and he now draws his letter to a close with a series of general issues addressing life in their individual congregations. He and the other New Testament writers often use traditional catechetical material in their letters, such as on submission to government in Romans 13:1–7 and 1 Peter 2:13–17 and on trials in 1 Peter 1:6–7 and James 1:2–4. This is the case in this section as Paul covers the same material in Romans 12:9–18 as he does here in verses 12–22. Paul has incorporated early church teaching on church life and practice here, but he has not simply copied it wholesale. Rather, he has closely examined the situation at Thessalonica and selected certain issues that are still "lacking in [their] faith" (3:10), then addressed them here. The point for us is that this is material the early church thought to be critical for the successful life of their churches. So we should pay very close attention to the implications of these exhortations for our churches today.

## PAUL ASKS FOR LOVE AND RESPECT
## FOR CHURCH LEADERS (5:12-13)

Since Paul and his team were forced to leave earlier than planned and severe persecution existed almost from the beginning, these churches were forced to grow in a crucible of hostility under young leadership. This probably meant that leaders had to emerge quickly and decisively to give guidance in these difficult times. He begins not with a command but a request, probably because of his great affection for these people. The verb for "asking" (*erōtaō*) is drawn from 4:1 ("we ask you and urge you in the Lord"), and here too the entreaty is combined with urgent exhortation that stresses the importance of the request.

It is essential that the members of the congregations give their leaders the support they need to lead them in these tumultuous times. Once more, he addresses them as "brothers and sisters" (see 5:4) to stress the atmosphere in which all this is lived out. They are affirming their God-sent leaders not just as a community or assembly but as a family of believers. The infinitive used here (*eidenai*) normally means "that you know," but in this context it means to "acknowledge" or "show respect to" the leaders. Some have debated which of these (acknowledge or respect) is better here, but aspects of both are almost certainly found in the message. They need to recognize and respect those God has chosen to lead them (as also in 1 Cor 16:15).

Paul notes three characteristics of the work of these leaders here. First, they "work hard among you," a term he uses often of those in ministry (Rom 16:6; 1 Cor 15:10; 2 Cor 10:15; Phil 2:16; 1 Thess 1:3; 3:5) to stress the diligent, hard work on their behalf. They are not just glory hounds who seek the attention of others but rather exert themselves to provide for the needs of their people. The people can trust them to do what is best and to extend themselves to benefit the church. They can be counted on to allow nothing that is needed to remain undone. Paul means this to be holistic, to include preaching and teaching in addition to management concerns and general ministry areas.

The second area of their ministry is to "care for you in the Lord." This is difficult to decipher, for there are two different meanings of *proistēmi*, one stressing authority ("rule, preside over, be at the head of"), the other stressing concern and aid ("care for, help, give aid"). Both are viable here, and Paul uses the word in both senses elsewhere (ruling in 1 Tim 3:4–5, 12; 5:17; aiding in Rom 12:8; 16:2). The interesting thing is that in the Roman world the two were combined in the "patron," a wealthy benefactor who both had power over and helped the client. Paul could easily have had this metaphor in mind, where the leader in the church both led and helped those who were under their ministry. The more I think about it, the more it seems to me that Paul intended both aspects and that they are interdependent here. This authority and care are wielded "in the Lord," namely, in the name of Christ and in his strength.

The third area is verbal, to "admonish you." *Noutheteō* simply means to "place something in someone's mind" and so can refer to positive instruction, but usually in the New Testament it has a negative connotation of admonition, and this is indeed its use in 5:14, to "admonish" or "warn" the idlers in Thessalonica. That is likely its use here in verse 13 as well, and it refers to their function as proclaimer of the gospel and the word, seeking to help the members to grow spiritually in Christ. Admonition is a necessary ingredient for growth, for we must rid ourselves of those factors in our life that hold us back. This is not a popular idea in our age of positive feedback and political correctness, but it is at the heart of true spiritual growth.

Respect for church leaders is not enough. The Thessalonian Christians must "hold them in the highest regard in love because of their work" (v. 13). The verb *hēgeomai* normally means to "think" or "regard," but in a context like this it means to "think highly of" or "esteem" another person. The two ideas to "respect" and "esteem" are close in meaning and refer to the high regard the leaders deserve in the community. This is especially true when he adds the adverb "most highly," a very strong adverb with three superlatives (*hyperekperissou*), literally "hyper-over-abundant" or "above and beyond all measure." This asks for the deepest honor and love possible for those God has given the church to lead and care for the people. Most think of obedience as the result of power and authority exercised over people. Not so here. Obedience results from love and esteem for the person giving the orders.

The means by which this highest possible regard is shown is "in love." Paul of course mandated love for all believers toward each other, and love was a particular distinctive of this church (1:3; 4:9–10), but it is especially to be shown the leaders for all the sacrifices they have made. The reason for all this loving reaction is "because of their work," summing up the three areas of their ministry from verse 12. Note that they are not given this esteem and love because their ruling positions demand it but because their own loving care deserves it. There was no "lording over" allowed in the church, as Jesus himself said (Mark 10:42–45). The leaders earned that love and respect by their own loving servanthood in exercising their office.

The last part of the verse, "Live in peace with each other," seems at first glance a separate issue, community harmony, simply added to the points discussed. Yet when love dominates, peace and harmony are the natural result. The saints are called vertically to love for those leaders who are above them and then horizontally to peace with those who are their peers in the church. There was pressure from outsiders (2:14; 3:4) and disquiet from inside, the result of the idlers in their midst (5:14; 2 Thess 3:15). They needed a decided unity and harmony to meet these difficulties.

## PAUL EXHORTS THE CONGREGATION TO MINISTRY (5:14)

As in 4:1, "we urge" introduces a new topic as Paul moves from a focus on church leaders to addressing the congregation as a whole.[1] The topic is the need to minister to troubled people with certain disorders in the church. These are not three actual groups, though the first may well be a particular group. Paul is still ruminating on those lacking in their faith from 3:10 and now names three types of people who need particular attention. By addressing them as "brothers and sisters" once again, he makes this a family matter as God's people seek to help fellow believers with particular spiritual problems to overcome their difficulties and get right with the Lord.

The first command is to "warn those who are idle and disruptive." This is the same verb for spiritual "admonition" used in 5:12 for warning people of problem areas in their lives. He labels this first group the *ataktoi*, a term that connoted two things, both likely part of the meaning here. These were "lazy" people who refused to work and remained "idle," and they were "disruptive" or "disorderly," refusing to heed the challenge of the leaders or the church to do their part and earn their keep. In the words of Ephesians 4:28, they were "stealing" funds from the church by forcing it to take care of them. Instead, they should "work, doing something useful with their own hands, that they may have something to share with those in need." Due to their refusal to work, they had turned themselves into the needy and had become quite disruptive to the normal life of the church. The NIV rightly translates both aspects, "those who are idle and disruptive."

It is possible they were clients of wealthy patrons in the church like Jason (Acts 17:6, 9) who demanded to be allowed to remain dependent clients and refused to contribute to the needs of the church or even to care for their own needs. It is also possible that they were eschatological enthusiasts who believed the Lord was

---

1. Some church fathers and others tried to make this a continuation to the exhortation about leaders in vv. 12–13, but the language of v. 14 doesn't really allow that. This refers to the ministry of all the "brothers and sisters" to one another.

going to return imminently and demanded to be allowed to quit their jobs and wait for him to arrive, thereby making the church feed them even as they looked down on them as less spiritual (see 2 Thess 3:6–12). We cannot know for certain.

The second command is to "encourage the disheartened." The verb means to comfort or console people who are troubled in their hearts. This rare term (*oligopsychous*, literally "small soul") refers to those discouraged and depressed, ready to give up. In the midst of all the pressures and persecution this church had experienced (see the introductory chapter), this is easy to understand. Some think it a result of the confusion about the fate of the deceased when Christ returns (4:13–18), and both are valid reasons for discouragement. These people need to be comforted regarding the final victory of God's people and encouraged not to lose heart.

The third command is to "help the weak." The verb (*antechō*) means much more than "help" but contains the idea of being "devoted to, attached to," a thing. This is not perfunctory help, simply doing our part for the common good, but an obsession for getting involved with "the weak." It is difficult to know whether these are the ill, the physically weak; or the poor, the economically weak; or outcasts, the socially weak. The majority of commentators think of these as the spiritually or morally weak, those who have fallen into sin, perhaps the same as the two groups at Rome, the weak and the strong, fighting over observing the food laws and the holy days (Rom 14:1–15:13). Paul seems to be speaking generally, so several of these may well be in mind. The main thing is the exhortation to deep pastoral involvement in the lives of those who are enduring these difficulties. From this we are all mandated to seek the gift of helps with respect to the needy, whatever the specific problem areas.

Finally, he sums up by ordering them to "be patient with everyone." The verb *makrothymeō* means to be "longsuffering" or put up with the foibles and even the sins of people, like God in the Old Testament (Exod 34:6; Ps 103:8; Joel 2:13). It is one of the fruits of the Spirit (Gal 5:23) and would transform the church today if people would be empathetic and tolerant of each other. It is a mainstay of true ministry and the only reason any of us are saved, for if God were intolerant he would have taken our lives long ago. We desperately need that same patience in dealing with fellow Christians.[2]

## PAUL MANDATES A REFUSAL TO RETALIATE (5:15)

When they are mistreated by others (again, persecution is probably in mind), Paul commands them to "make sure that nobody pays back wrong for wrong." The verb *orate* means "see to it, watch out and be careful." With all the animosity they are facing, they are strongly tempted to retaliate and "pay back evil for evil." This is the Old Testament *lex talionis*—"eye for eye, tooth for tooth" (Exod 21:24; Lev 24:20), but this principle is strongly restricted in the law. The famous command to "love your neighbor as yourself" in Leviticus 19:18 begins, "Do not seek revenge or bear a grudge against anyone," and this rejection of retaliation reverberates through both testaments (Ps 7:45; Prov 20:22; 25:21; Matt 5:38–48; Rom 12:17–20; 1 Pet 3:9).

Rather than seek to get even, Paul requires that believers "always strive to do what is good for each other and for everyone else." The word "strive" is *diōkete*, picturing great effort and hard work. It is not easy to return goodness for evil, but the Christian life centers on goodness and is known for good works. Peter states this well in his first letter: "Live such good lives among the pagans that, though they accuse you of doing wrong, they may see your good deeds and glorify God on the day he visits us" (1 Pet 2:12). The unbelievers, spreading lies accusing us of evil deeds, see our goodness, are placed under conviction by it, and are converted to Christ (also Rom 12:20–21). The two categories reflect Galatians 6:10, "let

---

2. Some have interpreted the "all" here to include non-Christians, but there is little indication of that. They enter the picture in the "everyone else" of v. 15.

us do good to all people, especially to those who belong to the family of believers."

## PAUL DETAILS THE CHARACTERISTICS OF THE CHRISTIAN LIFE (5:16–18)

Paul's brief commands here could have constituted a single verse, but Stephanus (who broke the Bible into chapters and verses in AD 1551) decided they were of individual importance, and he was right. Paul has been discussing social relationships in the church, but now he turns to the spiritual qualities that must character-ize the saints and selects three—joy, prayer, and thanksgiving. These represent the kind of life that pleases God and fulfills his will for us. The movement in this section is quite logical—from social responsibilities (vv. 14-15) to spiritual duties (vv. 16-18) to the work of the Spirit in prophecy (vv. 19-22). These are three crit-ical aspects of congregational life and apparently were areas in which the Thessalonian Christians needed to grow.

(1) "Rejoice always" (v. 16): At the very outset (1:6) Paul lauded these wonderful followers of Christ for responding to severe per-secution "with the joy given by the Holy Spirit." Then in 2:19-20 he twice called them "our joy." In other words, joy both characterizes them and is a gift they bestow on those who interact with them. They *are* joy and *bring* joy to all they meet. So this feeling of joy cul-minates in 3:9: "How can we thank God enough for you in return for all the joy we have in the presence of our God because of you?" Wow! What we wouldn't give to have this said of *our* churches.

The Christian life was never meant to be easy, but it has always been meant to be joyous. Throughout the New Testament joy is linked to the trials of life, as in James 1:2 ("Consider it pure joy ... whenever you face trials of many kinds") or 1 Peter 1:6 ("In all this you greatly rejoice, though now for a little while you may have had to suffer grief in all kinds of trials"). The key is that hardships force us to abandon all pretense of controlling our lives and to throw ourselves in utter dependence on the Lord. The joy comes not from the earthly situation (Heb 12:11) but from the realization that he is now in charge and turning things around for our best (Rom 8:28). The "always" especially has these times of difficulty in mind, and the Thessalonians epitomized this new attitude.

(2) "Pray continually" (v. 17): Prayer is that spiritual ingredient which turns sorrow to joy in trying situations. This is how we surrender to the Lord and express our utter dependence on him. Yet prayer also transcends personal needs and is to be expressed "constantly" (*adialeiptōs*), meaning in every situation and at all times. Prayer is communication with our Father, and we should never lose contact with him. The call to continuous prayer is a hallmark of his teaching (Rom 12:12; Phil 4:6; Col 4:2; Eph 6:18) and was a feature of his own life (Rom 1:9; Phil 1:4; Eph 1:16; 2 Tim 1:3). As a father, I cannot get enough calls from my children and grandchildren. This is how I need to relate to my heavenly Father, with a constant desire to "stay in touch" with him.

(3) "Give thanks in all circumstances" (v. 18): Prayer and thanksgiving are connected throughout Scripture, and expressing gratitude to God is actually a type of prayer, as in the thanksgiving hymns of the Psalms (individual—18, 30, 32, 34, 40, 66, 92, 103, 116, 118, 138; corporate—65, 67, 75, 107, 124, 136). Paul brings the two together often (2 Cor 1:11; Eph 1:15–17; Phil 1:3–4; Col 1:3), and so this is a natural extension of his basic philosophy of ministry. He considers it a spiritual obligation, saying in 2 Thessalonians 1:3 and 2:13, "We ought always to thank God for you," and so it is natural for him to mandate thanksgiving for all believers (as in Eph 5:4, 20; Phil 4:6; Col 1:12; 3:15). A heart of gratitude to God is especially critical in times of severe hardship, when it is necessary to remind ourselves of God's frequent interventions on our behalf in the past.

All agree that the closing comment relates to all three commands, not just this last one—"for this is God's will for you in Christ Jesus." As in 4:3, God's will is often linked with the moral and ethical lifestyle of his people (Mark 3:35; Rom 12:2; Eph 6:6; Col

4:12; Heb 10:36; 1 Pet 2:15) and always relates how one can please God (1 Thess 4:1). To exemplify a life of joy, prayer, and gratitude is to do the will of God and to please God. Moreover, this can only be done "in Christ Jesus": in union with Christ and under his empowering presence.

## PAUL DISCUSSES THE PLACE OF PROPHECY IN THE COMMUNITY (5:19–22)

Paul turns from three key spiritual qualities that should characterize believers to another issue in the Thessalonian church, another area "lacking in your faith" from Timothy's report in 3:10. Paul does not say what situation led to the necessity of this section, but it definitely developed out of the prophetic activity of the early church. Prophecy was one of the spiritual gifts distributed by the Holy Spirit, as in 1 Corinthians 12:7–11, "Now to each one the manifestation of the Spirit is given for the common good ... to another prophecy. ... All these are the work of one and the same Spirit, and he distributes them to each one, just as he determines." There were many prophets like Anna in Luke 2:36–38, Agabus in Acts 11:27–28, 21:10–11, or the four prophetess daughters of Philip in Acts 21:8–9.

Apparently there were prophets in Thessalonica, and their ministry caused tension in the church there. So Paul is addressing this in verses 19–22. Some think there was a backlash against this activity and that Paul is lending his support to the prophets and their ministry there. Others see the situation as the polar opposite, with people enamored of a prophetic movement, perhaps even one connected to the false prophets of 2 Thessalonians 2:2, who said the day of the Lord had already come. Of the two, the latter has more support in the text, but nothing can be proved. Paul seems to be calling for a balanced approach to the place of prophecy in the church, one that is open to the Spirit but not to any and every prophetic claim. So the key command is to "test them all" under the leading of the Spirit and every claim made, however frivolous it may be. Under the leading of the Spirit, they must decide which are truly from God. This is very similar to 1 Corinthians 14:39-40, "be eager to prophesy, and do not forbid speaking in tongues. But everything should be done in a fitting and orderly way." So he wants to encourage Spirit-directed prophecy and at the same time prevent excessive openness to fraudulent prophetic claims.

The structure is easily apparent, organized around two prohibitions (vv. 19-20) followed by three positive injunctions (vv. 21-22). Both likely describe problems in this area of charismatic activity. Some felt contempt for all attempts to prophesy, while others were uncritically accepting whatever they were told. The answer was to test each and every claim and decide which stemmed from the Spirit and which were lies and came from the top of someone's head.

### The Negative Side: Do not Quench Spirit-Inspired Prophecy (5:19-20)

The verb *sbennyte* was used for extinguishing a fire and can refer either to the total destruction of a thing or to a general restriction or prohibition of something. "Quench" is a perfect translation and probably refers to a cessationist movement in Thessalonica against Spirit-inspired prophecy. The grammatical form is called "present-tense prohibition" and means to "stop doing" something they have been doing, though it can also mean "do not at any time practice" something. One could say Paul was quenching their attempts to quench the Spirit.

Fire is a symbol of the Holy Spirit, as at Pentecost (Matt 3:11; Acts 2:3; 18:25; Rom 12:11), and Paul demands that the Spirit-fire be allowed to continue in the church. The Spirit is the guarantor and down payment for our final salvation (Eph 1:13-14), and it is a serious thing to curtail his presence and power in the church. They are not merely prohibiting individuals from exercising their prophetic fervor but acting against the Triune Godhead itself. As the author of Hebrews says, "It is a dreadful thing to fall into the hands of the living God" (10:31) and "For our 'God is a consuming fire'" (12:29).

To make certain they have caught this important message, Paul makes the prohibition more explicit in verse 20: "Do not treat prophecies with contempt." It is clear that several in this church believed the Spirit had given them the gift of prophecy, and for reasons we cannot know another group had decided this was not so and thus treated them with disdain. It is doubtful if this was as serious a situation as at Corinth, but it was serious enough. The church was in danger of serious conflict. It is doubtful that they were despising the Spirit himself, but they were definitely looking down on these practitioners, and that would result in real dissension in the church.

### THE POSITIVE SIDE: TEST ALL PROPHECIES (5:21–22)

Paul fleshes out the basic act in the first imperative with the two types of prophecies in the second and third imperatives. When you test a thing you differentiate between good and bad types. It seems the rejection of the prophets was ideological; all the prophecies were rejected as a whole group without testing them. So Paul commands, "test them all."

To be open to prophetic utterances does not mean to be naive and gullible and accept anything a person brings before you. Abuses by false prophets and false teachers were common in both testaments, and strong criteria were developed for separating the good from the bad. In 1 Corinthians 12:10 Paul speaks of the gift of "distinguishing between spirits," and in 1 John 4:1 we are told to "test the spirits to see whether they are from God, because many false prophets have gone out into the world."

The verb is *dokimazete*, calling for the examination of a thing to determine whether it is authentic or a fake. In trial passages, biblical authors use it of God's turning a trial into a test to prove the genuine faith of his people (Jas 1:3; 1 Pet 1:7). Here it is "all" those claiming to be prophets and "all" that they say that must be tested. It is both the person and the message that are tested for whether God has truly sent them and the Spirit truly inspired them.

Paul now explains the result of the examination, and the church has determined which are the "good" prophecies and which are the bad or "evil" ones. At the same time Paul tells them how he wants the church to react to both types. Those "good" (*kalon*) that are determined to be genuine prophecies sent by God and inspired by the Spirit are truly from the Lord and intended for the benefit of the church. They are to "hold on to" (*katechō*) those prophecies, a verb meaning to "hold fast, cling to, maintain possession of." This is an important verb in the New Testament, used for guarding and keeping key Christian truths (Luke 8:15; 1 Cor 15:2; Heb 3:6, 14). These are to be received as God's message to his people and followed with care.

Those prophecies found not to be from the Lord are to be deemed not just wrong but "evil" (*ponērou*). In fact, Paul has generalized this by saying "reject every kind of evil," placing false prophecies into a category of evil that stems from the dark world and is part of spiritual warfare. The verb is a cognate of the first verb, *apechō*, and means to "keep away from" or "have nothing to do with" a thing. Paul used it of abstaining from sexual immorality in 4:3. These are exceedingly dangerous because they are not just human lies but are demonically inspired falsehoods aimed at destroying God's work and defeating God's people.

## PAUL CLOSES HIS LETTER WITH FINAL GREETINGS (5:23-28)

Following **Hellenistic** conventions, Paul not only concludes his letter with the traditional prayer-wish (v. 23), closing doxology (v. 28), and greeting (v. 26) but also sums up some of the major themes, such as the call to holiness and the Christian walk (v. 23), God's work in their lives (v. 24), and the importance of brotherly love (v. 26). As such this forms a veritable summary of the letter.

## PEACE BENEDICTION (5:23)

A prayer-wish is a request for blessing from God for the recipients of the letter. Paul frequently culminates letters with a "God of peace" benediction (Rom 16:20; 2 Cor 13:11; Gal 6:16; Phil 4:9; 2 Thess 3:16) asking God (or Christ) to pour out his peace and blessings on the people. As such, it frames the letter with a call for divine grace and peace (with 1:1). This begins on a very high note, invoking "God himself, the God of peace." It is often thought that Paul chose the "God of peace" title on the basis of the conflicts in the church, but this is part of the traditional benediction formula (note the passages above), and Paul links peace here to the call for holiness in the prayer itself. God is characterized by peace and bathes the church in his peace through salvation in Christ.

This is not just a simple prayer for peace but expands it to include two interconnected requests: for complete sanctification and for final and holistic spiritual victory at the return of Christ. Both are themes that flow through the letter. While the call to a sanctified life comes especially in 4:3–4, 7–8 (part of the mandate to avoid immorality), it is also implicit in the work of the Holy Spirit and holiness in the first half of the letter as well, as in 1:5–6 (joy in the midst of suffering) and 3:13 (holiness in the presence of the Godhead). In many ways, holiness could be the defining theme, for the entire emphasis on living the Christian life by the will of God is an outworking of the process of holiness/sanctification. So to be children of the day, bathed in light (5:5), describes the sanctified life.

Paul's prayer is not just that we be sanctified but also that we become holy "through and through," translating two synonymous adjectives, *holoteleis* and *holoklēron*, both meaning "whole, complete." The first is with the opening clause and refers to complete sanctification, the second with the next clause, calling for the sanctifying process to affect the whole person—"spirit, soul and body." So this invokes complete sanctification for the whole person.

The second clause sums up the issues covered in 4:13–5:11, regarding the return of Christ, adding the challenge that when he returns we be found "blameless." This is the natural result of the first petition: when we have been completely made holy, our lives will be blameless or without fault, complete in him and wholly living the sanctified life. Paul is praying that the Spirit preserve us and keep us faithful to Christ, living in every area of our being for God. This virtually repeats the prayer of 3:13 that God strengthen them to be "blameless and holy in the presence of our God and Father when our Lord Jesus comes with all his holy ones."

The **parousia** has been central throughout this letter, beginning in 1:3, 10, with the emphasis on "hope" as "waiting for his Son from heaven." Then in 2:12, 16, there is a contrast between the saints, who are called "into his kingdom and glory," and the sinners, who are under "the wrath of God." The destiny of God's people is to be a "crown in which we glory in the presence of our Lord Jesus when he comes," to be blameless and holy at his return (3:13). This promise of the first half of the letter comes to full fruition in the second half, in the promise of the reunion of the deceased saints with those still alive when Christ comes (4:13–18) and the future of God's faithful followers at the day of the Lord (5:1–11).

Interestingly, this is a major passage in the debate over anthropology in Paul, for this is the one place he uses three terms for the different parts of human nature—spirit, soul, and body. The adjective "whole, complete" stresses the totality of our being. But many see in this a description of what makes up our being. The term for the debate is trichotomous (three-part) versus dichotomous (two-part) views of human nature. In 1 Corinthians 7:34 Paul uses two terms, "body and spirit," and Jesus spoke of two (Matt 10:28, "soul and body") or four parts (Mark 12:30, "heart, soul, mind, and strength").

This is in reality a false debate. None of the passages intend to tell *the* makeup of a human being, and the actual emphasis in all of them (as here) is on the completeness of God's work in us. The Bible actually divides the person into material and immaterial aspects, and we see this primarily in the intermediate state, where our material part is in the grave and our immaterial part is in heaven, awaiting the reunification of the person when Christ returns and every Christ follower is given their eternal or glorified body (1 Cor 15:42–54). So the point here is to stress our total transformation through the sanctifying work of the Spirit (his present work in us) and our final complete transformation when Christ returns (his future work in us).

## ENCOURAGEMENT: THE FAITHFUL WORK OF GOD (5:24)

Paul's prayer in verse 23 seems almost more than we can expect God to do, so he encourages the Thessalonians by ensuring that God will faithfully answer the prayer and do this great work in them. They need not worry about their own strength to achieve final sanctification nor the place of God in the process. Paul draws on the entire Old Testament in its emphasis on the *chesed* (lovingkindness) and *emet* (faithfulness) of God. In Deuteronomy 7:9 Moses declares, "The LORD your God is God; he is the faithful God," and Isaiah 49:7 states, "the LORD, who is faithful, the Holy One of Israel … has chosen you." Verse 24 may stem from this one in Isaiah. The promise here, in fact, is at the heart of the doctrine of the security of the saints, for in their weakness they can be assured of the power of God at work on their behalf (1 Pet 1:5). He will never fail those he has called to him, as in 2 Thessalonians 3:3: "The Lord is faithful, and he will strengthen you and protect you from the evil one."

## THREE REQUESTS (5:25–27)

These requests are connected only by the fact that they form an important part of the letter closing. Paul began this letter by praying and giving thanks for the Thessalonians (1:2–3), and now he closes by asking prayer for himself and his team. This demonstrates how close he has become to this young yet deeply committed assembly of believers. Prayer is a two-way street, and as he prays for them (v. 23), it is highly significant that they are praying for him.

The prayer request here is general, unlike others (e.g., Rom 15:31–32 or 2 Thess 3:1–2) where he has special prayer needs in mind. This is an important reminder regarding prayer. We should not pray only when there are important needs but should intercede for the daily needs and general spiritual situation as well. Prayer channels the presence of God more deeply into a person's life, and that in itself is critical enough. We all need prayer partners. Prayer changes things, and the more prayer that takes place, the more power we feel in our lives. Paul was a man of prayer, but this was not seen as magic to get things from God. Prayer is the natural reaction to God among his people! When love and sharing characterize a relationship, communication (prayer) will always take place.

Next, he requests that they "greet all God's people with a holy kiss" (v. 26). Greeting with a kiss was a very common Oriental greeting in the first century, seen in Jesus' time (Luke 7:45; 15:20; 22:47) as well as Paul's (Rom 16:16; 1 Cor 16:20; 2 Cor 13:12; 1 Pet 5:14). The emphasis here on the "holy kiss" is obviously meant to separate the Christian greeting from those in the secular world there, where it was somewhat perfunctory and meant to symbolize affection between people. For the church it was Christian love, and many believe it also signified peace and unity in the church. It was also done at times of reconciliation to symbolize the new oneness between former adversaries. It later took on eucharistic overtones and became a liturgical act.[3] Paul includes it in several epistles to encourage deeper unity and sharing among believers.

---

3. We might also note that in the Gentile world problems arose as it led to erotic affairs, and by the second century kissing between opposite sexes was no longer allowed.

On the other occasion Paul has "greet one another," while here he has "greet all God's people." Some see this as significant, calling the Thessalonians to reconciliation in light of some conflict in the church, with "all God's people" (literally "all the brothers") intended to represent those who have been wrongly excluded. This cannot be proved, but it must be recognized as a very real possibility here. The most likely situation would be the troublemaking idlers noted in 5:14 and 2 Thessalonians 3:6–13, but we cannot know for sure. For us this is a reminder that Christian love means reconciliation. It is amazing how many churches are split through interpersonal conflict between members, let alone theological disputes. Reconciliation and oneness must be a constant goal of church life.

The third request (v. 27) is to "have this letter read to all the brothers and sisters." This is a formal "charge," virtually demanding that they swear an oath to God that they will carry out his request. It was common to read publicly not only Scripture (1 Tim 4:13) but also apostolic letters (Col 4:16; Rev 1:3). This also switches from the first-person plural to the first-person singular, probably meaning Paul has taken the pen from the hand of his **amanuensis** or secretary and, following custom, is writing a final greeting in his own hand (as in 1 Cor 16:21; Gal 6:11; Col 4:18; Phlm 19). This is further evidence of the likelihood of some conflict behind both verses 26 and 27, as it all appears to reflect a serious situation.

With all the tensions represented in the issues of chapters 4 and 5, Paul had reason to demand that everyone in the church be read the contents of this letter. Since illiteracy was very high in the ancient world, this letter could not be just passed around, so he asks for a formal gathering in which every believer is required to be present at a reading of the letter. Most likely Paul was especially thinking of the idlers who had so far refused to adhere to attempts to reconcile them with the rest of the community. From 2 Thessalonians 3 we know this did not work either, so there is good reason to suspect that Paul especially had these people in mind here. However, he certainly wanted to make sure that all who were "lacking in your faith" (3:10) were present. His prayer was that all of the issues could be addressed and solved.

### CLOSING BENEDICTION (5:28)

Paul ends all of his letters with a similar grace-blessing that reiterates the opening greeting (1:1). This is exactly the same as Romans 16:20 and 1 Corinthians 16:23. Grace is what this epistle is all about, and without it nothing of any significance would ever be achieved. Everything of any eternal value we possess comes to us by the grace of God, and "the grace of Christ" especially signifies the blessings of salvation but in this context also includes the grace that will enable the Thessalonians to continue growing spiritually and solving the tensions that have troubled the community. The source of this blessing is "the Lord Jesus Christ," centering once more on his lordship (1:1, 3; 2:19; 3:11; 4:1–2). Paul is praying that Christ in his grace will drive the message of every part of this letter home to the hearts of the saints.

———

It is common to think that conclusions to letters contain little valuable content, and the relevance just peters out and disappears. That is decidedly not the case with Paul's letters, and the important material here almost keeps getting better. In the first section Paul provides a critical reminder of the importance of good leadership in the church (vv. 12–13). There are several books written on our times, exploring the burnout that underappreciated and overworked ministers too often have to face. Paul tells us that good leaders are to be treasured and allowed to function with full support and appreciation.

The rest of verses 14–18 speaks of different kinds of ministries God gives us to perform. The most difficult, as we will see in 2 Thessalonians, was to a group called the "idlers," a disruptive bunch who refused to work and expected others to take care of them. The value of this is to remind us that ministry is not meant to be easy and comfortable but rather to be life-changing and truly helpful to the needy. As we minister to each other and live the Christian life, three spiritual qualities should characterize us— joy, prayer, and thanksgiving (vv. 16–18). This will produce a vital church and please God. When these qualities are in control of the church, God is pleased and the Spirit is present.

Prophecy was an important part of the life of the church; through prophecies God gave specific instructions for the progress and ministry of a church. These were prevalent at Thessalonica but at the same time controversial, for a group was rejecting all prophecies as not from God. Paul takes a balanced approach, telling them not to quench the Spirit (vv. 19–20) but at the same time to test every prophecy to determine if it is truly from God (vv. 21–22). This has great relevance for our day when prophecy is just as controversial as it was at Thessalonica and cessationism is once again seen in an important segment of the church. I would follow Paul's approach here and be cautious yet positive.

The rest of the closing is also filled with relevant material for our day. In verse 23 Paul prays for God's twofold work in us; the present process of sanctification and the future victory that is ours at the parousia. That is at the heart literally of everything it means to be a Christian. This promise is anchored in the absolute faithfulness of God (v. 24), who will carry out everything he has promised. The three requests of verses 25–27 that bring this letter to a close show Paul's pastoral heart, for he is deeply involved with this church in his heart and desperately wants to heal its problem areas. His desire is that love and unity take control of these people, and he is doing everything he can to get the troubled members to listen and heed the challenges. May we all be as concerned as he for God's healing of troubled hearts in our churches.

# 2 THESSALONIANS

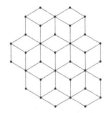

# INTRODUCTION: GREETING AND THANKSGIVING
## (1:1–12)

In spite of the fact that problems in the Thessalonian church have mandated a second letter, Paul is still very pleased with these people and with the way they have grown in Christ. His opening greeting is virtually identical with the first letter, including the senders/authors (Paul, Silas, Timothy), the recipients (the church of the Thessalonians in God the Father and the Lord Jesus Christ), and the greeting ("Grace and peace to you"). To avoid redundancy, I will not repeat the commentary proper and will allow readers to peruse the earlier chapter for exegetical comments.

Several summary points can be made. Paul is the author, as in the first letter, but the other senior members of his team are part of the nucleus, and both letters have likely resulted from their lengthy discussions of the situation there, so they are listed as co-senders. The oneness of his team is a valuable model for pastoral staffs in our day. It is also clear in all of Paul's letters that the people of God has expanded and become a "new Israel" with the addition of believing Gentiles to believing Jews, forming a new "olive tree" or church of God (Rom 11:17-21). The continuity with Israel of the old covenant era is quite apparent.

## PAUL GREETS THE THESSALONIANS (1:1–2)

Here we see two additions to the opening of 1 Thessalonians. First, God is presented as *"our* Father," emphasizing God as *abba*, the intimate, loving Father who cares for us and protects us. The Lord's Prayer (Matt 6:9, "Our Father in heaven") and Jesus' teaching in general secured this central theme, and it reverberates through the letter openings (Rom 1:7; 1 Cor 1:3; 2 Cor 1:2; Gal 1:3; Eph 1:2; Phil 1:2; Col 1:2; Phlm 3). God is not only the Father of Jesus Christ and of humankind in general, but of each of us individually, and this means that our salvation has made us the family of God.

The second distinction from 1 Thessalonians is in the greeting, where here he has added his characteristic "from God the Father[1] and the Lord Jesus Christ." This is implicit in the first letter but explicit here. It is clear that the Godhead is involved in this church. The Spirit is not named but is implied throughout. The Thessalonian church is a trinitarian operation, and the power and vigilance of the Triune Godhead are behind every part of it. We are not on our own in the Christian life, and we must rely on all that they are doing on our behalf. This also has critical implications for the doctrine of Christ as the God-man, the one who became God incarnate in human flesh, who was the very voice and presence of God, the **Shekinah** (the indwelling presence of God) that walked planet earth! This is a very auspicious beginning for any letter.

## PAUL PROVIDES A THANKSGIVING
## AND PRAYER (1:3–12)

This is a three-part message. Paul begins by thanking and praising them for their continuing growth in the Lord in verses 3–4, then encourages them that they would be vindicated and their persecutors punished in the end (vv. 5–10), and finally exhorted to live worthily of God (vv. 11–12). These people had been through a lot,

---

1. "Our" is added in some ancient manuscripts but most likely was not part of the original.

forced to be on their own way too early when persecution led to the flight of Paul and his team to Berea then Athens in Acts 17:13–16. They had to develop their own leadership and learn how to endure severe persecution, and yet they flourished through it all and became models for others to emulate (1 Thess 1:4–10). This spiritual growth continued, and so Paul once again lauds them for their accomplishments.

## THANKSGIVING FOR THEIR GROWING FAITH (1:3–4)

Ancient letters proceeded from author to recipient to a greeting followed by a thanksgiving and prayer. Paul follows this here but elaborates, since the **Hellenistic** thanksgiving was brief and somewhat formal. Paul's is warm and functions as an introduction to the contents of his letter. There is also an unusual addition not found elsewhere, as he uses the language of obligation, "we ought [*opheilomen*] always to thank God." This form is repeated in the second thanksgiving of 2:13 but nowhere else in Paul's thanksgivings, and it has occasioned some discussion. Some have said the Thessalonians were embarrassed by the effusive praise of the first letter and thought themselves unworthy; others think Paul had even been accused by opponents of deliberately flattering them. There is no hint for either view in the text here, and both are speculative.

More possible is the view that the author (some even think this a separate author) decided to be more formal and distant in this letter, but that founders on the reality that Paul is just as warm toward them in the rest of this letter as he was in the first one. The most probable explanation for this is that Paul is taking a normal Jewish approach by stressing the fact that the Thessalonian faithfulness makes him even more desirous of praising them. He feels obligated to God to make their wondrous response known to all. Far from being more distant, he was virtually inflamed with the *necessity* to thank God for them. He could not be grateful enough in light of their faithfulness and spiritual growth. The note of

continual gratitude ("always ... for you") is common (Rom 1:8;
1 Cor 1:4; Phil 1:4; and others) and reflects his prayer life, as he
regularly prayed for his "brothers and sisters" in the family of
God. He adds, "rightly so" (Greek, "as is fitting"), adding emphasis to his earlier "ought." The first stressed the divine obligation
behind his thanksgiving, this the human appropriateness of it in
light of their exemplary conduct. Both before God and before man,
such gratitude is completely mandated.

The reason is the same as in the first letter and is twofold:

1.  It is right "because your faith is growing more and more."
    In the first letter faith is part of the spiritual triad of faith,
    love, and hope (1:3; 5:8; see also 1 Cor 13:13; Gal 5:5–6; Eph
    4:2–5; Col 1:4–5) and is comprehensive, referring not only to
    their trust in Christ but to the content of their faith as well.
    Here it is not only spiritual reliance on Christ but also ethical
    faithfulness in their walk. The verb for "growing" is unusual
    (*hyperauxanō*), emphasizing the intensity of the abundant
    growth. Moreover, it is an ongoing intense explosion of
    faith and has not ceased. Since the events of the first letter
    (see 3:6), their trust in Christ and commitment to faithful
    Christian living have not abated but have grown even greater.

2.  It is right since "the love all of you have for one another
    is increasing." This was also stressed in 1 Thessalonians,
    seen in their ministry throughout the province (1:3, 8), in
    Timothy's report regarding their love (3:6; see also 3:12), and
    especially the praise of this very thing in 4:9–10. Like their
    faith, their brotherly love also continued to grow. Paul is
    encouraging them to center on these two key aspects of
    their church life to prepare them for the issues of the end of
    the age and the man of lawlessness in 2:1–12 and the prob-
    lem of the idlers in 3:6–13. They will need all the faith and
    love they can find when those issues hit.

In the next verse (1:4) Paul applies this faith and love to the
external situation of their persecution at the hands of their

opponents in Thessalonica. He wants them to know that he not only lauds them to their face but also boasts of them everywhere he goes. As he said in 1 Thessalonians 1:7, they have become exemplary "models" of faithfulness that all the other churches can follow, and he wants them to know this is still true. It is quite effusive—"your perseverance and faith in all the persecutions and trials you are enduring." They are undergoing terrible difficulties from both within and outside the church, and they are steadfastly enduring them all and remaining firm for the Lord.

The actual text states emphatically, "we ourselves [autous hēmas] boast," and this has led several scholars to think Paul is contrasting his bragging here with either his normal tendency not to boast or with others around (saying, "I am boasting far more"). However, this is unlikely, and Paul probably simply wants to make his pride in them doubly emphatic—"we ourselves owe it to the Lord to thank him and be proud of the wonderful work he has done in you." His team is bursting at the seams with joy over the way the Thessalonians have triumphed spiritually over their extreme hardships. It is a very public boasting; he brags of them virtually in all "God's churches" he visits.

The present tense throughout stresses as well as the use of "all" make it clear the opposition did not cease when Paul and his team left for Berea but continued to the present time and seemed unceasing. He uses two terms to describe their troubles—"persecutions and trials," once more emphasizing the intensity of the mistreatment. The pagans are throwing everything they have (short of martyrdom) at this young church, trying to eradicate it forever.

## ENCOURAGEMENT: VINDICATION AND JUDGMENT (1:5–10)

### Just judgment: their vindication (1:5)
Will all their sacrifices and suffering be worth it in the end? Paul spells out the answer in no uncertain terms. It is hard to imagine anything more encouraging than knowing the justice of God

and how it will make up to them everything they are enduring for Christ. Paul presents it to them in a courtroom setting, with the "evidence" laid out before them "that God's judgment is right," *dikaias*, meaning not only "correct" but even more "just." This is the theme of the book of Revelation, a "theodicy" (defense of God) proving the absolute justice of God's judgments.

There is some question as to what exactly constitutes the "evidence," and in the developing statement here it appears to be not so much their endurance but the "persecutions" themselves. This relates to the doctrine of the "messianic woes" of Colossians 1:24; Revelation 7:10-11 that God has instituted a certain amount of suffering that his messianic community will undergo in a "participation in [Christ's] sufferings" (Phil 3:10), and when that limit is reached, the end will come. As in Philippians 1:27-28, then, persecution becomes a "sign" to the pagans of their coming destruction and a "sign" to the believers of their coming salvation. God's judgment is indeed just, for in the words of 1 Peter 4:17 it "begins with God's household" in the persecution that is part of God's plan but will end with the final judgment of the enemies of God and his people.

The present result of this process is that they "will be counted worthy of the kingdom of God, for which you are suffering." The sufferings they are enduring are the blows of the sculptor's hammer fashioning out of the lump of rock that is their lives a masterpiece of creation, a God-worthy warrior of the divine kingdom. God is the implied agent wielding the hammer and creating something magnificent out of all their troubles. The picture is of the process of troubles involved in this new creation. It is the now and not-yet of the inaugurated kingdom that is in view, and it involves not only their present vindication but also their future glory. So their present suffering is a positive event in which divine judgment is already proving itself *dikaios*, just and right.

*The two aspects of divine justice (1:6-7a)*

Paul restates the basic premise, "God is just," and then establishes the two sides of his justice, punishment upon evildoers and "relief" for those enduring the hardships, called by many scholars the **"eschatological** reversal." God is at heart a "holy" God; holiness is his core attribute. This can be subdivided into two interdependent aspects, his justice and his love, and these together define his holiness. He is a righteous God, and justice and righteousness are the same term, *dikaiosynē*, and constitute the basis of his actions. This justice is a hallmark of all of Scripture (Gen 18:25; 1 Kgs 8:31-32; 2 Chr 6:22-23; Job 8:3; 34:12; Ps 7:8-11; 35:24; Isa 5:16; Zeph 3:5; Rom 2:6-8; 2 Cor 5:10; 2 Tim 4:8; Rev 18:6-7; 19:1-2).

As such, his justice demands first that he "pay back trouble to those who trouble you." This principle is called *lex talionis*, "the law of retribution"—what you do to God's people he does to you. God's suffering people can be comforted with the fact that theirs is temporary and will lead ultimately to their glory while their persecutors will suffer eternal "trouble" or "affliction" (*thlipsis*). The verb for "pay back" is *antapodounai*, at times a commercial metaphor for paying back what has been earned. Here it is judicial, meaning just recompense for crimes committed. The persecutors are standing before the judgment seat of God, hearing the recital of their misdemeanors and receiving the punishment they have earned with their nefarious deeds. The theme is reciprocity, and the absolute justice of the penalty is uppermost (Exod 21:23-25; Ps 137:8; Isa 63:4; 66:4, 6, 15).

The suffering faithful will see the opposite result (v. 7a). However, rather than reward, Paul stresses that God will give them rest: "relief to you who are troubled." Paul has made the two verses exactly parallel to emphasize the contrast between "affliction" (*thlipsin*) and "relief/rest" (*anesin*). This second term speaks of relief from affliction and is the perfect term for this context. In the present time there is animosity and opposition resulting in persecution and affliction, yet while there is no promise of present relief there is the guarantee of future and final relief, and this includes not only rest from the affliction but also the honor and glory that will be ours for eternity.

## The day of judgment defined (1:7b–9)

Paul now explores the timing of the day of judgment. It will take place "when the Lord Jesus is revealed from heaven in blazing fire with his powerful angels." The **parousia** ("coming") of Christ is found in 1 Thessalonians 2:19; 3:13; 4:15; 5:23 and in this letter at 2:1, 8. The focus shifts from God the Judge in verses 5–7a to Jesus the Divine Warrior, and his coming here is not for the catching up of the saints in 1 Thessalonians 4:13–18 but the destruction of the sinners from 1 Thessalonians 5:2–3. The event is the apocalypse (*apokalypsis*, "revelation"), and its origin is "from heaven." The world does not know him or recognize him, but this is a public manifestation of stupendous dimensions, and the world will know him then and quake in fear. He is not just Jesus Messiah or Great Prophet but Lord Jesus, and his supreme authority will be on display for all to see. He has been in heaven with the Father and Spirit from the time of his ascension, but now he will appear visibly on earth once more.

Two further descriptions are added. "In blazing fire" has a slight textual problem. Various manuscripts reverse "fire of flame" and "flame of fire," but the meaning is the same either way. The background stems from Exodus 3:2 (the "flame of fire" at the burning bush) and Isaiah 66:15 (the coming of the Lord "with fire," rebuking "with flames of fire"). Elsewhere fire is associated with the destruction of the world in 2 Peter 3:7, 10, and with eternal punishment in Revelation 20:14–15. The judgment awaiting the enemies of God and his people is as fearsome as it gets. This is an apt metaphor in light of the burning of cities that always accompanied ancient warfare.

The Divine Warrior is coming "with his powerful angels," considering the heavenly host as the armies of heaven, far more invincible than the Roman armies could ever pretend to be. There is some debate whether "power" should be linked with Christ (the angels of his power) or the angels themselves (as in the NIV), but this doesn't matter in the end, for power is invested in both. In Revelation 19:19-20 there is no battle. Christ and his heavenly armies arrive, and immediately it is over. The defeat is absolute and eternal in its ramifications.

In verses 8-9 Paul centers on the reasons for eternal punishment (v. 8) and the punishment itself (v. 9). At the divine tribunal the verdict is reached, and punishment is mandated by two factors: (1) they "do not know God," which as in Romans 1:18-19 is not due to human ignorance but deliberate suppression of the truth about God known both from God's creation and from human conscience. This echoes Isaiah 66:15-16, where God "executes judgment" with "fire and sword."

(2) They "do not obey the gospel of our Lord Jesus." Some think this a separate group, with the Gentiles those who do not know and the Jews those who do not obey. But the Jews are often described as not knowing God (Jer 4:22; Hos 5:4), and in this context the two are better seen as synonymous and describing all sinful humankind. Refusing to obey the gospel means both to refuse God's salvation and to live a life of sin. They intellectually reject the truth and ethically refuse to live God's way.

In verse 9 we see the penalty inflicted on them. Paul's emphasis throughout has been on the absolute justice that lies behind the severe penalty the sinners receive. The unsaved have flaunted God's justice and mocked his love, so God is giving them what they have earned for these actions. The picture of the tribunal continues as now Paul hands down God's sentence for the dire deeds done. Paul gave a double description of the crimes committed, and he provides a double penalty:

First, they are "punished with everlasting destruction." Paul uses a classical expression for legal decisions, with NIV's "punished" actually meaning "pay the penalty" or "suffer the consequences" (*dikēn tisousin*) for what they have done. This legal penalty is "eternal [NIV 'everlasting'] destruction" (*olethron aiōnion*), which could be meant literally of the total annihilation of all the enemies of God and the destruction of their world, or metaphorically of the disaster and terrible punishment awaiting them. There are aspects of both here, and Paul could well be thinking of the fiery destruction stated in 2 Peter 3:7, 10. The idea of eternal punishment—punishment that will never end and has eternal consequences—stems from Jesus (Matt 12:32; 18:8; 25:41, 46).

Second, they will be "shut out from the presence of the Lord and from the glory of his might." This in many ways is more terrible than the first, for it constitutes eternal separation from the presence of God and all the goodness that stems from him. The wicked will be totally immersed in evil and be forced to live entirely within its sphere. This is unimaginable in its severity. In Isaiah 2:10, 19, 21, the enemies of God and his people cower and flee from "the fearful presence of the LORD and the splendor of his majesty," while here they are forever separated from it. The "glory of his might" refers to his Shekinah glory and power that dwelt (Hebrew: *shakan* = "dwelling") with his people and mediated his divine presence. There could be no greater contrast than this eternal isolation from God compared to the blessed promise that God's people "will be with the Lord forever" (1 Thess 4:17; see Rev 21:3–4). The horror of this punishment is beyond belief—no contact with God whatsoever and immersed entirely in the absolute filth of all the evil in the world!

### The reward and glory for the saints (1:10)

The sinners receive their just deserts, and so do the saints. The judgment of the wicked will take place "on the day he comes to be glorified in his holy people." Of course, all this does not take place within one twenty-four-hour period. The "day" is the time of his appearing. While the calendar will differ depending on your view of the relation between the return of Christ and the defeat of the forces of evil, I am post-tribulation (see comments on 1 Thess 4:13–18) and so see this as the order of events: When Christ returns, he will reunite the living and the dead among his followers and give them their resurrection bodies (1 Thess 4:13–18; 1 Cor 15:51–53). At that time they will join with heaven's angels and form the army of the Lord (Rev 17:14; 19:14) and come down to earth with Christ to defeat the antichrist and his army at the Battle of Armageddon (Rev 19:19–21). This then is followed by the millennial reign of Christ (Rev 20:1–10), at the end of which will come the great white throne judgment, where the sinners are cast into the lake of fire and begin their eternal destruction (Rev 20:11–15), and the onset of the eternal reign of Christ with his saints (Rev 21). The "day of the Lord" of 1 Thessalonians 5:1–11 embraces all of these events and is depicted as a single "day" of **apocalyptic** time.

The focus here is on Christ more than on the saints. Some of the Thessalonians were filled with anxiety that they might miss the day (this was behind 1 Thess 5:1–11 as well) and needed to be assured of Christ's faithfulness to them. We will see this in the next chapter as well. It is hard to know why they were so confused and uncertain, but they were. In the next chapter the culprit will be a false prophecy, but here it seems to be more general. It may have been simply doubts about the assurance of their salvation. At any rate, Paul wants to comfort them that they need not worry and doubt. Their future is certain.

Christ will first be "glorified among the saints" (NIV "glorified in his holy people") taken from Psalm 89:7 LXX (the Septuagint), which speaks of God "glorified in the council of the holy ones" (Hebrew and NIV "feared"), namely, the angelic council of heaven. Paul uses it of the saints (the term is used of both in Scripture). He will come in his glory and reveal his glory to the world, and the saints will share in that glory (and receive their glorified bodies—see Phil 3:21). When we combine this with verse 9, we will share that glory, while our persecutors will be defeated and forced to acknowledge the glory of Christ and of us on that same "day."

Second, he will come "to be marveled at among all those who have believed." There is an inaugurated sense in all this, as God's people have "already" marveled at him when they first believed but have "not yet" marveled fully, for that will take place at the parousia. It is hard to imagine the wonder we will feel as we are caught up to meet the Lord at his coming. Paul wants to be sure this clears up their confusion so adds, "This includes you, because you believed our testimony to you," referring to their response to the original presentation of the gospel to them. Becoming a Christian is not a complex affair and does not demand extended catechetical study. Simply believing the gospel and turning our lives over to Christ is sufficient, and he wants these doubts removed and replaced with assurance of salvation on the basis of belief in Christ.

## PRAYER THAT THEY MAY BE WORTHY (1:11–12)

Paul thanked God for the Thessalonians in 3–10, and now he tells them about his prayers for them. "With this in mind" looks at the apocalyptic material of verses 5–10. In light of the fact that they are awaiting relief (v. 7) and glory (v. 10) when Christ returns, while their persecutors await eternal destruction (vv. 7b–9), they need to live a life worthy of their calling (v. 11). Future promise carries with it attendant present responsibilities, and Paul is exploring these.

This picks up on verse 5, where Paul began the paragraph on the justice of God by saying, "God's judgment is right, and as a result you will be counted worthy of the kingdom of God." The phrase "worthy of his calling" here thus means, worthy of his call to enter the kingdom of God. This could be a prayer that when they stand before God and give account for their lives (Heb 13:17; 2 Cor 5:10), they will be found worthy. However, it is even more a challenge to live worthy lives in the here and now, with the force more present than future. In this they depend entirely on God, who alone can make them worthy by supplying the strength and the guidance via the Spirit. The verb often means "count/consider you worthy," and some think that is the thrust here, but the context favors God as the acting force who will "make you worthy."

The second prayer flows out of the first one. The means by which God will make them worthy is that "by his power he [will] bring to fruition your every desire for goodness and your every deed prompted by faith." "Bring to fruition" is plērōsē, "bring to completion, finish," and refers to God's work in us. It is the same idea as in Philippians 1:6, "being confident of this, that he who began a good work in you will carry it on to completion until the day of Christ Jesus." God's is the enabling power to find victory over the flesh and the world's temptations (1 Cor 10:13), and he is absolutely faithful in giving us the strength to carry on and live the life God wants.

There are two areas in which we need that divine strength—the internal and personal desires (desire for goodness) and the resultant external actions (every deed prompted by faith). We always act on the basis of our inner wants, and Paul prays that God will control the process and give us strength to live rightly before him as a result. The first phrase is literally "desire of goodness," and while some might see this as God's desire, it is more likely their desire that is in view. Another issue is whether the thrust is objective (desire to do good) or subjective (desire prompted by goodness). This second view would see their desires stimulated by a life of goodness, and on the basis of parallels with the second phrase, most recent commentators opt for this. God and the Spirit perform their sanctifying work in us, and the life of goodness that results urges us to alter our internal desires to conform with his.

The second phrase is literally "work of faith" and is also generally understood subjectively, "deed prompted by faith" (as NIV). Consider the progression of the thought here. As God gives us power, our good walk with him stimulates our desires, and they lead to a deeper faith commitment, which in turn prompts our own labors to be in conformity with him. In other words, our goodness gains control of our desires and produces a deeper faith, which in turn stimulates our actions to be in keeping with his will. In doing so, God is bringing to completion his work in us and producing followers who are living the victorious life.

In verse 12 Paul provides two purposes (*hopōs*, "so that") behind the prayer of verse 11. First, God brings his work to completion "so that the name of our Lord Jesus may be glorified in you." This is an allusion to Isaiah 66:5 (also echoed in vv. 8–9 above), where the enemies of the righteous have mocked and challenged, "'Let the LORD be glorified, that we may see your joy!' Yet they will be put to shame." This echoes that passage, for here too the enemies of God's people will be put to shame as the Lord's name is glorified, and we share in that glory.

It is important to note the added "in you." We might assume that the glorification of Christ is future and will take place at his second coming, as is the emphasis in verses 5–10. But the wording "may be glorified in you" adds a present emphasis. The message is that Christ is glorified in the goodness and faith-based works of the Thessalonians (v. 11) that are defining their present walk with the Lord.

The second purpose is that "you [may be glorified] in him, according to the grace of our God and the Lord Jesus Christ." As Christ is glorified in us, we are enabled to share that glory as a result of the grace of God and Christ. There is an inaugurated sense in which we are in process of sharing his glory in the present as a foretaste of the final glory we will have with him when he comes again. Our glory has begun in the gift of the Spirit and will be culminated when we take our place in eternity at the side of the Triune Godhead.

There is debate over the proper translation and meaning of "the grace of our God and the Lord Jesus Christ." The same definite article governs both God and the Lord in the Greek, and this leads many to translate it "the grace of our God and Lord, Jesus Christ"

(NLT, ISV, marginal in GNT, NIV), thereby emphasizing the deity of Christ. This is quite possible, but in the context God and Christ are acting together, and I must agree with the majority of recent scholars and say both God and Christ are in view here. Thus the NIV translation is preferable.

---

This opening chapter of the second letter, like the first, follows normal Hellenistic letter-writing procedure and forms an opening prayer and thanksgiving. This is quite heartfelt, for Paul feels very close to these people and has an abiding love and respect for them. There are three parts, each of them quite relevant for us. First, verses 3–4 laud them for their continually growing faith and love. The mission team is positively gloating over the wondrous growth of their faith in Christ and love for the saints, and they want these people to know they brag to all the churches around about the work of God among these people. It is great to see Christians so deeply involved with each other, and the church today needs to follow this cohesion and unity—we see far too little of this in our time.

The second part (vv. 5–10) leads us into the apocalyptic truths that are equally important for us today. These faithful saints are undergoing terrible persecution and suffering, and God is telling them that this is all part of a larger plan for their eternal reward, with their enemies bound for the penalty of eternal destruction and punishment they have earned on the basis of their evil deeds. The saints, however, will find both relief and reward for all they have endured. The fiery punishment inflicted on sinners is mandated by their deliberate rejection of the truth (they know it but refuse to heed it) and their resultant disobedience to God and the life he mandates. They will not only have everlasting punishment but also be forever separated from God and his goodness. They will be immersed in the filth of sin and evil for all eternity. The righteous, on the other hand, will share the glory of Christ and be filled with wonder (the unsaved will be filled with terror) as his glory (and ours) are revealed to the world when he returns.

The final two verses of this section (vv. 11–12) define the Christian life that results from this. As God brings his work in us to completion, he reproduces his goodness in us, and that stimulates our desires to conform with his. This in turn deepens our faith, leading to good deeds that magnify him. The purpose of this is that the glory of Christ is manifest in us as we faithfully live for him. The glory of the saints is both present and future, and our sharing of his glory in the here and now is but a foretaste of the eternal glory that awaits us.

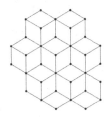

# THE DAY OF THE LORD AND THE MAN OF LAWLESSNESS
(2:1–12)

M any of the Thessalonians were beside themselves with despair, as a false prophecy had convinced them that the Lord had already returned and they had missed it. This would mean not only that they would be left out but also that their very salvation was forfeit. In refuting that dangerous error, Paul has given us one of the more difficult passages in his letters because several of the details are found only here, and he does not explain them all that deeply. So we have to do the best we can. The Thessalonians desperately needed pastoral intervention, and the situation demanded that they receive comfort. Paul's argument is quite simple. The **parousia** cannot have already occurred, for before it can come certain events must take place, and those events have not taken place. The result, however, is quite valuable, for we learn several things we would not have known otherwise. Let us get started.

## PAUL EXPLAINS THE FALSE REPORT (2:1-2)

Paul first presents the topic: "Concerning the coming of our Lord Jesus Christ and our being gathered to him." This of course was also the topic of 4:13-18, but the problem differed there, as a group at that time was worried that those saints who had died would not be around to be "caught up." This concerns the other side of the parousia: the end of this world and final judgment. Everything in this letter is related to the parousia event, as every aspect of the eschaton (the end of human history) flows from it. In fact, it is virtually synonymous with the "day of the Lord" (1 Thess 5:2; 2 Thess 1:10), which it initiates.

The issue clearly relates to the timing of the parousia. The Jewish people expected one "coming" of the Messiah, and it was intimately connected to the restoration of the nation, often called their "regathering" (Ps 106:47; Isa 27:13; 52:12; Zech 2:7). Jesus spoke of this regathering in connection with his own parousia (Matt 24:31; 25:31–32). Paul clearly picked up on Jesus' teaching in his many references (1 Thess 2:19; 3:13; 4:15; 2 Thess 1:7, 10).

Apparently teaching had come "allegedly from" Paul and his team that "unsettled" and "alarmed" many in the Thessalonian church. The word "unsettled" means to be "shaken," and several have translated it "scared out of their wits." We see the reason in the rest of the verse: "asserting that the day of the Lord has already come." This probably means they connected that "day" with the outpouring of God's wrath rather than the coming of Christ to gather the saints, and that the fact that they missed the "rapture" meant that they were under the wrath. This teaching was similar to 2 Timothy 2:18, where some false teachers said that "the resurrection has already taken place." So they had missed it, and all that remained was wrath.[1] In the Old Testament the day of the Lord was associated with final judgment (Jer 46:10; Ezek 30:2–3; Joel 1:15; 2:1). This led to terror on their part.

---

1. Some take the perfect tense "has come" as referring to an imminent or impending return rather than a return that had already taken place, but it is hard to see why this would frighten them so severely. The view above is more likely.

The source of the message is apparently unknown. Paul writes that it may have come through "a prophecy or by word of mouth or by letter." The main thing is that it did not come from Paul and was patently false. Prophecy was fairly common in the early church, as seen in Agabus (Acts 11:27–28; 21:10–11) and the discussion of prophecy in 1 Corinthians 14. So the Thessalonians were completely open to prophetic claims and accepted this particular prophecy without question, even though its message conflicted so starkly with what they had been taught. This provides a valuable lesson for us today. We need to be Berean Christians who "examined the Scriptures every day to see if what Paul said was true." Truth is in the word, not in the musings of any one teacher or prophet. I have often thought that a preacher with charisma could lead nearly any church around into heresy within two to three years and lose hardly anyone. We need to be more Bible-centered and truth-based than we tend to be.

## PAUL NOTES THE EVENTS THAT MUST COME BEFORE THE DAY ARRIVES (2:3–12)

### THE REBELLION AND THE MAN OF LAWLESSNESS (2:3–5)

Paul declares the person who related the message a false prophet when he says, "Don't let anyone deceive you in any way." These people are deceivers who deal in falsehood, and they must be opposed. "In any way" looks back to the three possible sources of verse 2. Whichever form it came in, it was a false prophecy. The claim that it came from Paul was a lie. "Anyone" who presents future **eschatological** teaching that conflicts with the official Christian doctrine already taught to them is spreading falsehood and must be opposed. So this is a stern rebuke to the gullible Thessalonians for listening to such erroneous reports. To prove this, he appeals to his previous teaching (v. 5) that two preliminary events will precede the coming of the day: "that day will not come until the rebellion occurs and the man of lawlessness is revealed."

This twofold scenario is not found anywhere else in Paul. The relationship between the two is unclear. The Greek has the rebellion occurring "first" (the NIV translates it "until"), but there is no "then" before the second clause and most commentators surmise that the rebellion and the appearance of the man of lawlessness are simultaneous, and that "first" may well modify both. This lawless individual will instigate the rebellion and rule over it. In this sense these two events must occur "first" before Christ's return. Also, there is a conditional (*ean mē*, "if not" or "unless") without any content, and many have called this a "missing apodosis," or conditional clause. But it is best to supply the content as "that day cannot come," and the NIV translation ("that day will not come until") is perfectly apt for this.

The "rebellion" is *hē apostasia*, "the apostasy" (the definite article "the" indicates a technical term for an **apocalyptic** event) predicted by Christ in the Olivet Discourse (Mark 13:5–7, 21–22, and parallels). There is both a political (rebellion) and a religious (apostasy) sense to the word, and both are indicated here. In Judaism there was a firm tradition regarding a segment of God's people who would rebel against God at the time of the end of history (1 Enoch 91:3–10; 93:9; Jubilees 23:14–23; 2 Baruch 41:3; 42:4). Such a flocking after false teachers occurred often in the early church (1 Tim 4:1–5; 2 Tim 3:1–9; 2 Pet 3:3–4; 1 John 4:1–3), and the "apostasy" here is the final one of this lengthy string. So Paul is describing the final rebellion that will pave the way for the coming of the man of lawlessness. It involves the rejection of God and Christ, and people turning themselves over to the cosmic powers behind this figure. In other words, it is first a rebellion against God and second an apostasy from the true religion.

Paul's designation of the personification of evil and rebellion as "the man of lawlessness" is probably not a technical title but a description of his nature, "the one who rebels against God's laws." He will be a figure "revealed" by God and sent by Satan to lead the final rebellion, and he is called by John "the antichrist" (1 John 2:18, 22; 4:3; 2 John 7) and "the beast" (Rev 13:1–8; 19:19, 20). He will be the culmination of all the false prophets and teachers down through history and will appear in the last days. The idiom "son of" or "man of" stresses the primary characteristic of an individual, so this describes him as the one who denies there is any divine law to control sin and rebellion. To follow him is to live a life without God and in opposition to his will.

He is further described in similar terms as "the man doomed for destruction" (Greek, "the son of destruction"). Actually, there is disagreement over this. The actual phrase could mean "the one who will be destroyed" or "the one who will destroy." Those who opt for the latter often connect this with the ancient extrabiblical book Psalms of Solomon 17:11, which reads, "The lawless one laid waste our land so that no one inhabited it; they destroyed young and old and their children together." This was a depiction of Pompey, the great Roman general who "laid waste" to Palestine in 63 BC. While possible, a more likely background is found in Daniel 7:8; 8:9, the "little horn" of Daniel, which supplied background also to the beast of Revelation 13. Moreover, the destruction image of apocalyptic tends to be passive, depicting the destruction of the evil powers by God. That is likely the thrust here as well. The NIV paraphrase is correct; his doom is certain; he will be destroyed by Christ, the Divine Warrior, when he comes.

In verse 4 Paul further describes the earthly actions of the man of lawlessness. He is the emissary of Satan who in Revelation 13 is part of the counterfeit trinity (the dragon, the beast, and the false prophet, Rev 16:13) and will lead the Satanic attempt to destroy the people of God. There is a double strategy of the powers of evil here. First, "he will oppose and will exalt himself over everything that is called God or is worshiped." This in itself was sufficient to prove that the day of the Lord could not have come, for no such figure had arisen yet. However, this is just the beginning, for Paul took the opportunity to expand on this theme and provide them (and us as well) with major teaching regarding the final rebellion of the forces of evil.

The opening description is the key. He is the enemy of all that is good and "opposes" everything that has anything to do with God, and he is the epitome of arrogance, "exalting himself" over everything that is of God. Both are comprehensive and concern "everything that is called God or is worshiped." In other words, his entire purpose is to lead all the world in rejecting God and replacing him with himself as the pretentious claimant to deity. In Revelation 13:2–8 the dragon (Satan) gives the beast (the antichrist) his own power and authority (not God's!), and he uses that authority to get all the earth-dwellers (the sinners) to worship him. This is exactly the picture here, as this lawless one/antichrist supplants not only the one God of the Jews and Christians but all the gods of the pagan world as well. His goal is to be recognized by all religions as the god of all. This goes beyond the imperial cult, which made the emperor one of the gods. He will come across (and actually pull it off!) as the goal of all of earth's religions, and for this brief period he will actually unite all the religious longings of every religion in himself.

The second strategy is presented as the result (*hōste*, "so that") of the first: "he sets himself up in God's temple, proclaiming himself to be God." This builds on Daniel 11:36, which predicts a future king who will "exalt and magnify himself above every god" (see also Ezek 28:2–10). This picture of an apostate king who makes the Jerusalem temple his throne room was first fulfilled in Antiochus Epiphanes, who thought himself to be the son of Zeus and caused the Maccabean revolt by setting up altars to Zeus in the temple (and villages of Israel) in 167 BC. Second, there was Pompey, who entered the holy of holies in 63 BC; and third, the insane emperor Caligula, who in AD 40 sent an army to place statues of himself in the temple but was assassinated before the command was carried out. Finally, in AD 70 at the destruction of Jerusalem Vespasian's son Titus entered the holy of holies just before his armies leveled the temple.

The term for "temple" here is *naos*, meaning the sanctuary itself containing the holy of holies. This evil figure takes over the *bēma* or throne of judgment reserved for God alone in the holy of holies. He will then proclaim the greatest lie ever uttered in the history of this world, that he himself is God.[2] Paul is not saying the antichrist will actually be a Roman emperor. In Revelation 13 the emperor Nero is the primary figure after which the beast is modeled, yet the beast/antichrist is not Nero but a Nero-like figure. It was very common, after the emperor Augustus named his revered uncle Julius Caesar a god, for Romans to consider their emperors one of the gods, and in the time of Domitian it had become one of the Roman cults labeled "the imperial cult." The picture here builds on that image. The lawless one will set himself up as world ruler and then god of this world.

A major debate has developed out of this picture. Many consider this a literal prophecy and have developed a prediction regarding the literal rebuilding of the Jerusalem temple in our time so that the antichrist can make it his throne. However, I would follow those who see this as typological teaching to depict the antichrist setting himself up as both emperor and god of this world. Paul is using the theme that came down to him from Daniel to the Maccabean revolt in order to portray the actions of this Satanic being. This is an apocalyptic portrayal using language symbolically and not just literally to picture the event. The debate on this comes up again and again in passages like Jesus' Olivet Discourse (Matt 24–25 and parallels) or Revelation.

---

2. Some have tried to take *naos* here not as the Jerusalem temple but figuratively as the church, and the picture is of a false prophet leading the church into apostasy. However, this doesn't make as much sense in this apocalyptic context as the literal picture we have seen here of the antichrist proclaiming himself in the temple to be God.

Paul reminds them in verse 5 that this is not new material: "Don't you remember that when I was with you I used to tell you these things?" Note the rebuke encased in this question. They should never have been misled by this false prophecy, for they had more than enough knowledge to unmask the falsehood that the day of the Lord had already come. On several occasions Paul reminded them of things they had already been taught (1 Thess 2:9; 3:4; 4:1; 5:1–2), and he does so again here. He switches to the first-person "I" to stress that he was the source of that knowledge, and so they had no excuse for the memory loss that led to so much distress when they accepted the false teaching. Moreover, the imperfect tense *elegon* means that he "used to tell them" this on several occasions. It was not a peripheral point made once and easily forgotten. This crisis should never have happened.

### The Restraining of the Man of Lawlessness (2:6–7)

This is a most difficult portion, one of the toughest in the New Testament, for Paul provides no background and there are no biblical texts that discuss a restraining force. I wish I could have been there when he had taught on this, so it is impossible to decide for certain. A few things can be said, and I will explore several possibilities. Paul presents both a restraining force (v. 6 in the neuter) and a restraining person (v. 7 in the masculine). It fits into the category of verse 5, as he begins, "And now you know what is holding him back, so that he may be revealed at the proper time."

The Satanic power behind the figure is already working hard against God and his people (v. 7), so the question is why this person has not appeared. Paul answers that the restraining force is currently still in charge so that he cannot appear. This force is ensuring that he not arrive until "the proper time," undoubtedly that time when the Lord returns and the day of the Lord arrives. This lawless one will initiate the final events at the end of history, so he is not allowed to come until that God-chosen time is here. Note the interplay of present and future in this. The future is imminent, not here yet, and fighting to come. The reason it cannot is that the present restraint is in control and keeping the future at bay. This force ensures that the power of lawlessness cannot gain control and produce this figure before his appointed time. The imagery is all apocalyptic and centers on God's control of salvation history to bring all events to fruition at the time he has designated. Satan is trying to wrest control from God but failing due to the restraining force.

Paul addresses the topic of spiritual warfare in the added clause "for the secret power of lawlessness is already at work." The term for "secret power" is *mystērion*, an apocalyptic word for divine truths that have been kept hidden or secret but are now being revealed to God's people. Remembering that lawlessness here means rebellion and rejection of God and his laws, it is not that this Satanic opposition has never been understood but that the revelation of how it is to be manifest in these last days is now being uncovered for God's people to see. God is laying bare his strategy and methods; he is in control of them; and they are under God's supervision. Satan's strategy will come to light at God's pace and in the way that God wishes. This secret war is "already at work" in this world but curtailed. It is not allowed to finish what it has started.

Now in verse 7 the restrainer is a person rather than a thing. The emphasis is that he is at work "now" in the present. The lawless one is future because the restraining one is controlling the present. This restraint will continue until "he is taken out of the way." At the appointed time in the future he will be removed, and the divinely sent obstacle will be gone, allowing this figure to emerge and the final events to begin.

The options for identifying this figure are as follows:

1. Many church fathers thought this was the Roman Empire and the Roman emperor who sought to restrain evil, but that does not fit the facts of the first century, when much of the persecution came from Rome, which personified the evil power and not the realm of goodness.

2. This could be meant more generally of civic government and the rulers who oversaw life in it. But this is a religious rather than civic issue, and the lawlessness was against God's laws, not civil laws. Government was my choice for many years, but I find it unlikely now.

3. Many think the restraining force is the proclamation of the gospel and the restrainer the apostle Paul. Yet if this were true, Paul would be prophesying his own death, and that does not seem likely. He apparently believes he will be among those alive at the parousia according to 4:13–18.

4. Another form of this is that the force is indeed the preaching of the gospel, and the individual is an angel of God, for many Michael, the archangel-protector of God's people in Daniel 10:13, 21; 12:1. The main problem with this is that although Paul links them closely, they are nevertheless two separate entities. So others take this as Michael in what he does and who he is; that is a more viable alternative.

5. A very popular view among dispensationalists is that the two refer to the Holy Spirit, with the neuter referring to *pneuma*, the neuter noun for "Spirit." While the Spirit himself is viable, building like this on a neuter noun seems far-fetched and doubtful. So many have made the force to be the church, with the Spirit removed when the church is raptured, caught up to heaven. The problem here is twofold: it only works if the pre-tribulation rapture is correct, and even then there is no other passage that teaches the removal of the Holy Spirit for the tribulation period. In the end this is too speculative.

6. Others have seen the restraint as brought about by evil, the "power of lawlessness" in verse 7, and Satan, who passes on his authority to the lawless one and then is removed. But the removal of Satan is very unlikely. The antichrist will rule under his authority, not after that authority has been removed.

7. The restraining force is the plan of God for ending the
   world, which is the contents of the scroll of Revelation 5
   and 10, and the being is God himself. Throughout these two
   verses, every detail has related to the appointed time set
   up by God, and the lawless one will only come when God's
   plan comes to fruition. It is "taken out of the way" by being
   fulfilled. The purpose of the enigmatic language is apocalyptic symbolism.

My preference is for number 7, with numbers 3 and 4 next
most likely. Number 3 is viable if the individual is not Paul but the
preachers of the gospel in general. Whichever we prefer, the primary message is that the Lord cannot have come, for the restraining force over evil is still in operation, and the lawless one has not
been revealed. The great rebellion/apostasy and the man of lawlessness are future events that must precede the return of Christ
and only then will initiate the day of the Lord.

## THE COMING OF THE MAN OF LAWLESSNESS (2:8–10)

### His coming and ultimate end (2:8)

Paul wants to deepen their knowledge of this important event and
so goes into more detail about the coming and end of this evil lawless being, this son of Satan and chairman of the joint chiefs of
staff of the evil empire (presented as such in Rev 13). When the
restraining force is "taken out of the way," Satan will act and send
this being. In Revelation we have the "great imitation" theme, an
ongoing parody in which the dragon/the devil will parody God's
perfect work in detail after detail. One of these found here as well
is the parody of the parousia of Christ with respect to the "revelation" of the antichrist (man of lawlessness) as he comes to earth in
order to "deceive" or "lead astray" the world of sinful humankind
(compare Rev 12:9; 20:3 for the dragon and 13:3–4 for the beast).

This revelation will be a significant turning point, for it will
mark the true beginning of the "great tribulation" (so called due

to Rev 7:14, "these are they who have come out of the great tribulation"). He is presented as a human being who is completely possessed by Satan and becomes his personification on earth.[3] The early church saw this "tribulation period" as the seventieth week of Daniel (Dan 9:24–27, and so a seven-year period), with the "covenant" or truce broken in the middle by the little horn. This end of the covenant coincides with the "revelation" of the true identity of this figure. He had deceived the world and come across as a man of peace, a holy person who was solving the world's crises and bringing peace to the world. The revelation of his true nature and purpose will put an end to that folly, but the world will still flock after him. This revelation will likely consist of a worldwide proclamation that he is uniting all the nations of the world under his empire and amalgamating all the world's religions under himself, with the "false prophet" of Revelation 13:11–18; 16:13 as the head of the one-world religion and himself with his father Satan as the gods of the new unifying religion.

The ultimate destruction of the lawless one is portrayed two ways. First, the "Lord Jesus will overthrow [him] with the breath of his mouth," built on Isaiah 11:4, where the branch of Jesse "will strike the earth with the rod of his mouth; with the breath of his lips he will slay the wicked." This is a frequent theme, the destruction of the enemies of God and his people with the very breath of God (Isa 30:27–28; 1 Enoch 14:2; Psalms of Solomon 17:24–25; Rev 19:15). All ancient religions had a "god of the storms" (for instance, Baal), and the image was quite natural for destruction, as the tornadoes and hurricanes we see every spring and summer can attest.

Second, Christ "will destroy [him] by the splendor of his coming." The verb for "destroy" is *katargeō*, a favorite of Paul to

---

3. This assumes we accept the antichrist figure and the tribulation period as literal and not as purely symbolic. Those who prefer the symbolic understanding will see this as a metaphorical retelling of the power of evil in our world. Interestingly, very few (if any) of the commentaries on the Thessalonian letters see this as metaphorical.

describe the nullifying or rendering powerless of the old self. Here it intensifies that to total destruction. The picture is the end of the antichrist's power and of his very existence on earth. In Revelation 19:17–21 this will occur in the aftermath of the final battle, when he and the false prophet are cast into the lake of fire. This final defeat will take place "by the splendor of his coming," using two nearly synonymous terms, *epiphaneia* ("appearance, manifestation") and *parousia* ("coming"), with a growing consensus that the two are combined to stress the glory and wonder of the second coming (thus NIV's "splendor"). An epiphany is a manifestation of a ruler's power and glory and is often coupled with the defeat of his enemies. In the exodus the **Shekinah** (the glory of God dwelling among his people) had a military function, going before the nation and protecting it day and night (a pillar of fire by night and a cloud by day, Exod 13:21–22), and here the glory of Christ at his coming plays a similar role.

### The Satanic deceits that lead to death (2:9–10)

When this lawless antichrist comes in his counterfeit parousia, it "will be in accordance with how Satan works," with deception and total animosity toward all who are duped by his tactics. Paul spells out these tactics and purposes in these two verses. First is his use of "all sorts of displays of power through signs and wonders that serve the lie." The event itself looks to the breaking of the covenant in Daniel 9:27. The lawless one will enter the temple, declare the worship of God and Christ a capital crime (Rev 13:14–15), and establish himself as emperor and god of the earth (much in the manner of Roman emperors).

He will cement his rule and the universal worship he demands with "displays of power" (see Eph 6:12: "the powers of this dark world"), utilizing "signs and wonders" to anchor "the lie" that he is the legitimate ruler and god of this world. These supernatural miracles will be real but still counterfeit because they merely copy the truly God-sent miracles of Christ. Moreover, he will authorize the false prophet, the third member of the counterfeit trinity, to perform these same miracles in his name and so "deceive the inhabitants of the earth" (Rev 13:13–14; see also 16:14; 17:8; 19:20b). They are "signs" because they demonstrate the true nature of the one performing them, and "wonders" because the whole world is filled with astonishment and flocks after the lawless one.

In verse 10 Paul tells us the ultimate results of the "ways that wickedness deceives": the eternal destruction of those who fall into its snare. It does not take any lengthy proof to certify the deceptive power of sin. A simple documentary of people vacationing in Vegas will more than suffice. It comes across as harmless fun, a period of freedom where we get to say "what happens in Vegas stays in Vegas," with the picture of a person returning home fully refreshed. The ruined lives are conveniently ignored.

Paul's emphasis is on "all the ways that wickedness deceives," namely the fact that evil uses every type of deception there is. Sin is omnidirectional in its tactics, using every possible trick to seduce its mark and gain control. Its deception is used in the service of seduction, and the ultimate goal is destruction. At the same time, the objects of the deceptive work are unbelievers, who are already "perishing" and are headed for final judgment. The goal is to complete the process, to gain absolute power over the unsaved and move them further and further from God and the life of salvation he offers.

The reason why these people are perishing is part of Satan's strategy of deception. They "refused to love the truth and so be saved." The truth is clearly the gospel that Paul proclaimed to the Thessalonians and that led to their conversion, but the world of sinful humanity had rejected the truth of the gospel and preferred the lies of Satan, the father of lies (John 8:44), because they wanted to reject the truth. They were not simply ignorant of the truth and sadly deceived by the lies. They had no desire or love for the truth and deliberately chose to follow the lies. Such is the power of depravity. Thus it is not just that they will not be saved; they do not *want* to be saved! It is not that the world does not want eternal life. Rather, they want it on their own terms and do not want it God's way. The eternity they want is the Roman kind, an eternity of sensual pleasures realized after a lifetime of the same.

## THE RESULT: DIVINE JUDGMENT (2:11–12)

This is present judgment rather than final judgment, as "God sends them a powerful delusion so that they will believe the lie." This doesn't sound fair. Satan deceives the unsaved with his lies, then God anchors that by deluding them into believing those lies. What chance do they have? Where is the justice in that? Yet this is a major biblical theme, explained well in that major passage on depravity, Romans 1:18–32. Humanity knew the truth and deliberately rejected it, so God "gave them over" to their sins (Rom 1:24, 26, 28) so that they suffer the consequences of their folly. That is the case here as well. They have rejected the truth of the gospel (v. 10b), so God has turned them over to the lies of Satan.

It is a "powerful delusion," stressing its supernatural origin and its irresistible nature. The term for "powerful" here is *energeia*, often used for the "working" of God (Eph 1:9; Phil 3:19; Col 2:12). The "energy" of God is always powerful! This happened in the Old Testament when God would send malignant spirits to delude the fallen nation (1 Kgs 22:19–23; Ezek 14:9). In a sense this passage contains another "deluding spirit" sent to anchor the lost in their sin. Since they are going to "believe the lie" told by the lawless one, let it take place at the direction of God and perform his will. Thus in reality they fall into God's trap, and the antichrist is his tool. They reject the truth of the gospel of Christ and believe the lie of the antichrist. Due to the high-handed nature of their rejection, God gives up on them and deepens their rejection. Their doom is certain.

The result (*hina*, "so that") is eternal "condemnation," a judicial term for the sentence handed down when guilt is proved in the courtroom. Paul already provided the sentence itself in 1:8–9:

"punished with everlasting destruction and shut out from the presence of the Lord." He also tells us the twofold basis of the condemnation here. They have been proved guilty of an evil mindset (they "have not believed the truth") and of the evil actions that flow out of this (they "have delighted in wickedness"). Paul already stated the first part in verse 10 ("they refused to love the truth"). This is a description of their pretense that they can show contempt to the truths of God and get away with it. The term for "wickedness" is *adikia*, and both parts of the Greek word are part of the thrust here—"not [*a-*] right [*dik-*]." "Wickedness" is "not right" and is itself the lie. When they embrace and rejoice in wicked behavior they are following the delusion.

Sin is the Satanic delusion that will dominate the final period of history when the devil's great emissary rules. The "lawless" nature of the world at that time does not mean total anarchy but rather rebellion and rejection of God's laws. The antichrist will have laws, *his* laws, but the central feature is that wickedness will reign. The entire world will be Las Vegas, and hedonism will be the rule of the day. However, this worldwide triumph of sin over goodness will last only so long as the antichrist is on the throne. The time period is that of the seventieth week of Daniel, with the antichrist on the throne only for that period. At the end of it Christ comes back, and the utter annihilation of the army of the beast as portrayed in Revelation 19:17–21 ends that period, leading to the "condemnation" of final judgment as described in Revelation 20:11–15.

———

Paul wrote this passage because of another eschatological misunderstanding, caused this time by an erroneous report, a false prophecy that Christ had already come back. If this were true, the Thessalonians had missed the gathering up of the saints and so faced the wrath of God and final judgment. Paul disproves this by reminding them of what he had taught them earlier, that before Christ returned a personification of evil, a man of lawlessness, would have to come and initiate the final rebellion against God.

The future event portrayed in this passage is one that most of us have thought little about, for it is too confusing. Yet it is a very important passage, for it is the deepest depiction in Scripture of the reign of evil that will occupy that final period of human history when God will allow the cosmic powers of evil their last hurrah, their final attempt to control a world in which God is absent.

At the outset of that time (vv. 3-4 here) a figure will arise and begin to come to power, called "the man of lawlessness." He will combine political acumen with religious depth and begin to solve every crisis around the globe. As he brings peace to one hot spot after another, people will begin to clamor for him to take over. He seems to be the one kind of politician they truly want: a deeply religious man who can be trusted.

In Scripture this time period is linked with the seventieth week of Daniel 9:24-27, so this period is the first half, the establishing of the covenant when the antichrist comes to power. Here in 2 Thessalonians 2:6-7 we see that God, not Satan, is actually in control. It seems as if the evil cosmic powers are having their way, but in reality God, according to his plan, has been a restraining force, allowing the antichrist only enough room to gain power at God's designated time for God's designated period. He wanted power from the time of Paul on, but God would not allow it. God will remove his restraints only for the short period he has determined, called the "tribulation period."

In the middle of that "week," the restraining force of God's will is removed, and Satan is finally free to act. The lawless one accepts the pleas of all the nations, sets himself up as ruler of the world, and at the same time establishes a one-world religion with himself as the focus and the second beast of Revelation 13:11-18, the "false prophet" of 16:13, as the religious head. Thus begins the time of apostasy, the rebellion to end all rebellions. It is the closest the evil powers will ever come to winning, and it will only last three and a half years.[4]

John portrays what the antichrist/lawless one will do for this "tribulation period" in Revelation 13–16. He will declare Christianity an outlaw religion and execute all who refuse to take his "mark," presented as a religious tattoo that means you now worship the beast (13:16–17). It will be the most intense time of persecution and martyrdom in human history, but it will ultimately end in defeat. The emphasis here is on the complete annihilation of the lawless one and his followers by Christ when he comes (v. 8) and the extent to which the antichrist deceives those who join the apostasy by using visible "signs and wonders" to lead them astray (vv. 9–10).

In fact, God himself will anchor that apostasy by sending a "powerful delusion," giving them over to their rebellion and powerfully sending them into complete and final rejection of all that is God and Christ (vv. 11–12). These former members of the church who have gone apostate and joined the antichrist have deliberately cut themselves off from the truths of the gospel and have embraced a life of wickedness. Therefore they too will suffer everlasting condemnation.

Then Christ will return and with him the combined army of the angels of heaven and the saints with their glorified bodies. The reign of the antichrist will end with the total destruction of the army of the beast/antichrist and the casting of the beast into the lake of fire (Rev 19:17–21).

---

4. Described in Revelation as "forty-two months" (13:5; drawn from Daniel 7:25; 12:7), "1260 days" (Rev 11:3; 12:6; building on Dan 12:11–12) and "time, times, and half a time" (Rev 12:14; also from Dan 7:25; 12:7).

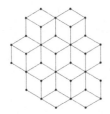

# FURTHER THANKSGIVING
# AND ISSUES
(2:13–3:5)

P aul has now completed the primary reason for the second letter, proving the false prophecy wrong and correcting their misunderstanding about the Lord's return and the coming of the day of the Lord. In the next ten verses he introduces some general issues before tackling the second reason for this letter, the problem of the "idlers" (3:6–15). After 1:3, 11, this also becomes a second section of thanksgiving (2:13–14) and prayer (2:16; 3:1, 5).

## PAUL THANKS GOD FOR THEIR
## ELECTION TO SALVATION (2:13–14)

This not only begins the following section; it also closes the preceding with the other side, not just judgment of the sinners but also the salvation of the righteous. This is emphasized by the opening "but" (de), establishing the contrast between the sinners and the saints. These suffering Christians can be assured of their complete vindication, encompassing both their own election to salvation but also the condemnation of their persecutors. So the scene has passed through the darkness of the destruction of evil and moved into the sunlight of their present and future salvation.

Paul begins with a second note on his obligation to thank the
Lord after 1:3. Once more he owes a debt of thanks to the Lord for
his amazing work among the Thessalonians. It is due entirely to
God's grace that the Thessalonians are not only "brothers and sisters" but also "loved by the Lord," almost certainly a reference to
Jesus since in Paul *kyrios* nearly always refers to Christ. So both
God and Jesus are involved in their lives and have chosen them for
salvation. This may well be an echo of a passage dear to Paul, who
belonged to the tribe of Benjamin. In Deuteronomy 33:12 Moses
blessed the Benjaminites, calling them "the beloved of the Lord."
Paul is passing this blessing on to the Thessalonians, showing once
more that Gentiles are part of the new Israel, the church.

The basis of his deep thanks to God is the fact that "God chose
you as firstfruits to be saved." Note the absolute antithesis between
God's response to the opponents and to the Thessalonians. He sent
them a "powerful delusion" to anchor their rejection of the gospel,
and he responds to the openness of the Thessalonians by electing
them to eternal salvation. If any of them are feeling doubts about
their salvation, it is time to discard all uncertainty and rejoice
in the security of their true relationship with God. God's choosing them for himself was a frequent emphasis in the first epistle
(1:4; 2:12; 3:3, 13; 4:3, 7; 5:9, 23-24), and he wants them to know that
their future salvation is not dependent on their own efforts but on
"God's power" that "shields" them as they walk the walk (1 Pet 1:5).

The rest of the phrase contains a major text-critical problem.
Ancient Greek manuscripts are divided as to whether it should
read "from the beginning [Greek *ap archēs*] for salvation" (codices א D Ψ, most minuscules, preferred in KJV, CSB, NASB, NET) or
"as firstfruits [Greek *aparchēn*] to be saved" (codices B F G P, preferred in NIV, NRSV, ESV, LEB). For a couple of reasons I will side
with the NIV and others, for Paul never uses *ap archēs* to mean
"from the beginning" (*archē* usually means "ruler" in Paul), while
"firstfruits" occurs often (Rom 8:23; 11:16; 16:5; 1 Cor 15:20, 23; 16:15).
The firstfruits signified the beginning of the harvest, and Paul

wants to encourage them that they are indeed the beginning of a great harvest for God in that region.

There is a twofold means (*en*) "through" which this salvation is procured. First, "the sanctifying work of the Spirit," the divine side, looks at salvation in its comprehensive sense, combining conversion, when the Spirit is given (Rom 8:14–17), with the process of holiness, which is effected by the Spirit. A few have seen this as the holiness that God places in the human "spirit," but that is extremely unlikely, for the work of the Holy Spirit in believers is a favorite topic of Paul. The point here is that our salvation is not complete until we have grown in the Spirit and been "set apart" for God. This is always the result of the Spirit's work in us (Rom 15:16; 1 Cor 6:11; 1 Thess 4:7–8; 1 Pet 1:2). The key to divine election is the gift of the Spirit, who empowers the work of God in us.

Second, "belief in the truth," the human side, details our response to the Spirit's work within us. This is the truth of the gospel, and the convert places her trust in the gospel presentation of salvation and turns to Christ. This is the reverse of verses 10–11, where the unsaved believed the lies of Satan. So Paul describes salvation as the work of the Spirit and the human response of faith to that Spirit-work within us.

In verse 14 Paul adds further imagery to his description of salvation in verse 13, saying that God "called you to this through our gospel, that you might share in the glory of our Lord Jesus Christ." He chose them (v. 13) and called them (v. 14). The third means (after the two in v. 13) by which they found salvation is "through our gospel," referring to their proclamation of the gospel when they first came in Acts 17:1–4. The message is that their salvation is of divine origin via the gospel of Christ, not of human origin via Paul. It is supernatural in scope and heavenly in essence.

The ultimate purpose (*eis*) of this calling is "that you might share in the glory of our Lord Jesus Christ." This repeats Philippians 3:20–21: "we eagerly await a Savior from [heaven], the Lord Jesus Christ, who … will transform our lowly bodies so that they will be like his glorious body" (also Rom 8:17–18). The literal statement is "for an obtaining [*peripoiēsis*] of the glory of our Lord Jesus Christ," which probably has the active sense of "acquiring" or "obtaining" something for one's self. Obviously we do not acquire the glory of Christ for ourselves but rather receive what God has given us. Certainly the primary thrust is the resurrection of the body at the return of Christ, but there is an inaugurated sense as well, as from the moment of conversion we actually share in the glory of Christ, as in 1 Thessalonians 2:12: "live lives worthy of God, who calls you into his kingdom and glory." We have begun the process and are already growing in glory (!) but await the consummation of our glory at Christ's parousia.

## PAUL COMMANDS THEM TO STAND FIRM (2:15)

Most of their problems and all of their misunderstandings dealt with in the two letters resulted from a failure to remember what they had been taught, and Paul had to exhort them again and again to bring truths back to memory in order to correct doctrinal and ethical errors (1 Thess 2:9; 3:4; 4:1; 5:1–2; 2 Thess 2:5). The opening "so then" in this sense refers back to all the material not just in this letter but in the first one as well, reminding them that if they had done so earlier a lot of problems could have been averted. This becomes a very important reminder to us as well. Ignorance of the teachings of the word and the church allows a great deal of difficulties to arise that with knowledge could easily be solved quite quickly. Theological awareness is even more important in our day, for there are so many more false teachings out there than at any time in the past.

Paul's command to "stand firm" (*stēkete*) is a call to doctrinal stability, to be deeply committed and solidly anchored in the truths of the word. He restates 1 Thessalonians 3:3, 8, when some in the church were "unsettled" or visibly shaken by their trials while the majority "stood firm." He then defines what he means in the next phrase, "hold fast to the traditions [*paradoseis*, 'teachings' in

the NIV] we passed on to you." These are the official apostolic traditions of the church, those statements formulated to help the members understand the truths received in Scripture from God. Good
examples would be the "received" traditions about the death and
resurrection of Christ in 1 Corinthians 15:3-8 or the words of insti-
tution of the Eucharist in 1 Corinthians 11:23-26. The Thessalonian
church received these official teachings either "by word of mouth
or by letter," that is, sometimes in actual teaching sessions with
Paul or another member of his team or in letters like either of the
two letters he sent them (including this one).

This is such an important point for us. When I turn the radio
to Christian stations, I sometimes hear teachings that leave my
mouth hanging open and asking, "Where did they get that from?"
Not the text! In our day many of us are Athenians, "doing nothing but talking about and listening to the latest ideas" (Acts 17:21),
and as a result some very bad theology is being passed on as "new
truths." The elders of a church are called to be "able to teach"
(1 Tim 3:2; 2 Tim 2:24), and that means being knowledgeable about
theology and able to help explain difficult *truths* to the congregation. Mainly, we must learn to *care* about theology. The sad thing is
that many of us think theology is boring and don't want to get into
it. In reality, truths such as those we have dug into in this chapter
regarding the way this world is going to end are hugely interesting and relevant. Theology can be boring, but then it is due to the
teacher, not the subject matter. We need to find the "joy of discov-
ery" in doctrinal areas.

## PAUL GIVES A PRAYER FOR COMFORT
## AND STRENGTH (2:16-17)

We now come to the first of the closing prayers, opening with a
lengthy description of Christ as "Lord Jesus" and of God as "our
Father," drawn from 1:1 to stress their lordship over this world
and their deep intimate relationship with us as part of the family
of God. The comfort stems from the Godhead, Father and Son

together. Interestingly, the two subjects, God and Christ, together have a single verb, suggesting an emphasis on the deity of Christ. He is not only Lord but God of all and one with the Father. In this sense, it is also important to note that Jesus is first in the sentence (in 1:1 God is first), adding further emphasis on Jesus in this strong christological context.

However, God is predominant as well, and the two clauses that follow modify him specifically as the one "who loved us and by his grace gave us eternal encouragement and good hope." His love and his grace are joined together as the single attribute (they are governed by a single definite article) of a God whose love led to his gift of grace. In Romans 15:4 Paul stated that the past Old Testament truths were written "so that through the endurance taught in the Scriptures and the encouragement they provide we might have hope." This is Paul's emphasis here as well. God's loving grace-gift to them is first of all "eternal encouragement" or "everlasting comfort," the perfect gift for a beleaguered people under intense persecution (1 Thess 1:6; 3:4) and full of fear in light of the false report that the Lord had already returned and they had missed it. But why "eternal"? Most likely the point is that God is going to take care of them not only in the present but also in the future right up to eternity. God will "never leave nor forsake" them (Deut 31:6, 8; Josh 1:5).

In addition God will give them "good hope," another in a long line of modifiers—"firm hope" (2 Cor 1:7), "blessed hope" (Titus 2:13), "better hope" (Heb 7:19), "living hope" (1 Pet 1:3). Hope is another of the major themes in these letters (1 Thess 1:3; 2:19; 4:13; 5:8), with so strong an **eschatological** emphasis in which we have "the hope of salvation as a helmet" (1 Thess 5:8). Paul may have used this phrase because it was a popular idiom in the Roman world for the "hope" of life after death, and this issue was one of the major sources of worry for these people, as seen in both epistles (see below).

The content of the prayer is in verse 17. It is fitting that he asks the God who encourages to "encourage your hearts." In

1 Thessalonians 3:2 Paul said he had sent Timothy "to strengthen and encourage you in your faith," and he continues that thought here. As elsewhere, both aspects of the word are part of its use here: God encourages by comforting them. Paul has explored the areas where comfort is needed in both letters—their severe persecution, the general suffering they have endured, the anxiety caused by their eschatological misunderstandings regarding the fate of deceased believers (1 Thess 4) and of all the saints of Thessalonica if they missed the return of Christ (2 Thess 2). This prayer is for us as well. Anxiety is a part of life. The one thing all human beings share is the uncertainty of life in a fallen world—things are always going wrong. For God's children, however, we know that in the end everything is going to work out for the absolute best—eternity with the Father, Son, and Holy Spirit! In the meantime, God superintends and comforts us in our hard times.

At the same time, we lack the strength to endure on our own, so in the very same area the second request is that the Godhead "strengthen you in every good deed and word." Note that the request is not just for strength to endure but for God's power that enables us to turn our difficulties around and transform despair into good deeds. Note that Paul stresses "in every good deed and word" (see also Luke 24:19; Rom 15:18; Col 3:17). In everything they say and in the action that flows out of this into what they do, may goodness be the capstone of their lives. Most likely, this prepares for the following section on the idlers in 3:6-15, who were useless in what they said and shiftless in what they did.

## PAUL PRESENTS CLOSING PRAYERS (3:1-5)

In all of Paul's letters, he closes the letter by asking prayer for himself and his team and prays to God for the recipients of the letter. He does this here as well, asking for prayer in verses 1-2 and praying for the Thessalonians in verses 3-5. As always, these prayers function also as exhortation, calling on his readers to live up to the content of the prayers. In the opening introduction to Paul's letters, his beginning thanksgiving and prayer always function as **paraenesis**, exhortation to put the contents of the letter into practice in their lives (see 1 Thess 1:3–10; 2 Thess 1:3–12). Now this closing prayer performs the same function, culminating these themes.

Yet unlike the earlier letters, it also provides a transition into the final exhortation of the letter regarding the idlers (3:6–15). This is highly unusual and difficult to understand. It is not a new issue just sprung on Paul, for he commented on them also in 1 Thessalonians 5:14. Most likely, Paul wanted this epistolary close to introduce the challenge of the idlers by commending the church for its positive response to the gospel and then trusting that they would continue to be obedient in the difficult issue of the idlers among them.

## REQUESTS FOR HIMSELF AND HIS TEAM (3:1–2)

Paul prayed for the Thessalonians in 2:16–17; now he asks them to pray for him. He and his mission team are in Corinth at the start of their difficult ministry there. No one had any idea how serious this request was that "the message of the Lord may spread rapidly and be honored, just as it was with you." The first request came to pass, as the church initially grew in similar difficult circumstances, just as it did in Thessalonica (Acts 18:1–11). But no church caused as much personal involvement and heartbreak on Paul's part as did the Corinthian church. With regard to their "honoring" the gospel, the opening vision God sent Paul after he was forced out of the synagogues says it all: "Do not be afraid; keep on speaking, do not be silent. For I am with you" (Acts 18:9–10). Paul would need the Lord's presence greatly in the years to come with this church!

"Spread rapidly" is the Greek "run" (*trechē*), a metaphor normally used for individual spiritual growth (1 Cor 9:24–27; Gal 2:2; Phil 2:16) and only here of the spread of the gospel. Still, it provides a strong image of the effort expended to proclaim the gospel and its swift ministry among the lost. It may well echo Psalm 147:15, which says God's "word runs swiftly" when he sends it to earth.

Victory in the games is a favorite background source for depicting the Christian life, and it is quite apt here. Yet the emphasis is not on our effort but on God's empowering presence. He alone turns the struggle into victory, and that is Paul's prayer.

The second request is that the gospel of Christ be "honored," using *doxazō*, "glorified," picturing the honor or glory the victorious runner receives after winning the race. The two images combined produce an image of Christianity competing with other world religions to win adherents. Here it is a prayer for converts. This was based on constant experience, as the gospel was often greeted with mockery (at Athens) or severe opposition (in nearly every city according to the book of Acts). A wonderful exception was at Antioch, where the Gentiles who heard the message "were glad and honored the word of the Lord; and all who were appointed for eternal life believed" (Acts 13:48).

Paul adds "just as it was with you," undoubtedly intended to encourage the Thessalonians about their own positive response to the gospel. Note that the emphasis is on their past response. Paul is hoping that this will continue in the difficult issue he has yet to address, the idlers among them. He is hoping that this positive example of past openness and obedience will continue and that the Thessalonians will help the gospel truth to "spread rapidly" among those troubled Christians too.

The next prayer request for Paul's team (v. 2) is "that we may be delivered from wicked and evil people," a reference obviously to the unsaved who have rejected both the gospel and the messengers who proclaimed it. This repeats the prayers of Romans 15:31 and 2 Corinthians 1:10-11, prayers that Paul perhaps more than anyone in history could justly utter due to the terrible amount of rejection and persecution he experienced (2 Cor 11:23-29). To me, one of the most amazing occurred at Lystra and Derbe in Acts 14:19-20, when they stoned Paul and thought he was dead (he must have been in a severe coma with no evidence of breathing), yet when they left he just got up, dusted himself off, and went back to the city, leaving the next day as if nothing had happened! I think a miracle had taken place! So this is merely another in a long stream of opposition, and Paul is much more concerned about the gospel than himself.

He adds "for not everyone has faith" probably to ask prayer not just for his deliverance but for the conversion of his persecutors. "Faith" here is not just trusting in Christ but the life of faith that results. Paul wants prayer that these people both find saving faith and begin living in faith as true believers.

## Encouragement and Request for the Thessalonian Faithful (3:3–5)

### Encouragement that the Lord is faithful (3:3–4)

The first two verses centered on the situation Paul and his team were facing in Corinth. Now he returns to the situation of the Thessalonians, and the first two verses are meant to be encouragement that God will not fail them in their current predicament. Paul is primarily addressing once more the persecution situation of the church there, and he begins with a contrast between the lack of faith on the part of the pagans and the absolute faithfulness of the Lord Christ,[1] "But the Lord is faithful, and he will strengthen you and protect you from the evil one."

There are two wordplays in this. First, they have no "faith" while Christ is "faithful," and second, Paul prays for deliverance from "evil" and promises them protection from the "evil one." The latter play on words highlights the antithesis between good and evil, and promises the triumph of good over evil. These are welcome words for a people under the gun, but they have to take the long view. There is no end in sight for the persecution, and we know that hatred and violent opposition will continue so long as

---

1. As I have pointed out several times, in Paul's writings "the Lord" nearly always refers to Christ.

this world exists. But that is just the point. This world is doomed, and we can be absolutely certain that evil's days are numbered.

The faithfulness of Christ ("the Lord" in Paul is nearly always Christ) to his people is another of the themes of these letters. Life will let them down, and their neighbors will turn on them. But the Lord will always be there and will do two things: First, he will "strengthen you," continuing the prayer of 2:16–17 that the Lord encourage and strengthen the people. In the context the prayer is to provide the strength to endure the evil actions of their neighbors against them, but it must also include strength to live the Christian life and defeat the many temptations all around them.

Second, he will "protect" or "guard" (*phylaxei*) them from "the evil one," or Satan. The picture is the Roman praetorian guard around Caesar to protect him from any danger that might arise. In the Psalms God "protects" his people (Ps 12:7; 41:2; 121:7), and this idea continues in the New Testament (Phil 4:7; 1 Tim 6:20; 2 Tim 1:12, 14; 1 Pet 1:5). The idea of protecting and delivering someone from Satan begins with the Lord's Prayer, "deliver us from the evil one" (Matt 6:13), and continues throughout the early church (John 17:15; Eph 6:10–12; 1 Pet 5:8). Attacks from Satan are frequent here (1 Thess 2:18; 3:5; 2 Thess 2:9). Spiritual warfare was seen as real back then, and we need to realize the truth of it in our own day.

To help them to realize his assurance that they were spiritually mature and could handle the pressure, Paul adds (v. 4), "We have confidence in the Lord that you are doing and will continue to do the things we command." This bridges from present to future obedience. Their present obedience stems from the commands of the first letter that they are keeping, and the future from the commands of this letter that Paul is confident they are going to keep. Probably he is especially thinking of the commands regarding the idlers of verses 6–15. That is a very difficult situation, and he wants to encourage his friends in Thessalonica to listen carefully and heed the instructions.

In the Greek it says, "we have confidence *in the Lord about you*,"
and that yields a critical point. Paul's confidence is not in them
per se but in the Lord, who strengthens them. We can do nothing
in our own strength but fail. In his famous passage on spiritual
warfare he says, "be strong *in the Lord* and in *his* mighty power,"
and so the key to victory is to "put on the full armor of God" (Eph
6:10, 13). As in the last verse, "the Lord is faithful," and we can be
assured of ultimate triumph if we put our trust entirely in him as
we go into battle against the powers of evil. He will always "provide a way out" whenever we are tempted (1 Cor 10:13) and give us
the strength to win through.

### Request that the Lord guide their hearts (3:5)

When Paul prays for the Lord to "direct your hearts," he is speaking of their walk with Christ and their ethical conduct. He wants
to be sure they are living by the will of God and that their goal is
to please him in all they do. The two areas where he wants to see
guidance are "God's love and Christ's perseverance." The first question is whether "the love of God" means our love for God or feeling the same depth and kind of love that God feels, or the experience of the love God has for us. This latter is the likely thrust, for
Paul's prayer is that the Lord guide them *into* (*eis*) God's love, that
they be immersed in the love he has for them. Earlier in 2:16 he
described God as the one "who loved us," and so this prayer is for
them to be completely enveloped in that love, to experience it at
the deepest level.

Another difficult decision is the exact meaning of "the endurance of Christ." It could mean that the Thessalonians endure
opposition and suffering while remaining true to Christ, but the
sense is more likely similar to the first phrase (the love of God),
that as they endure, they do so following the example of Christ,
who persevered in the face of incredible animosity and remained

faithful.[2] Putting the two together, Paul is asking that the Lord Jesus Christ direct their hearts so that they fully experience God's love for them and Christ's model of perseverance as they walk through life. Paul's hope is that the two areas will give them the strength to handle that most difficult issue, solving the problem of the idlers in their midst.

———

The material in this section centers on general issues in the church but still contains important material for us to consider. It actually would be a fine sermon, and could be called "What the Christian Life Should Look Like." There could be three main points:

(1) What it means to be the elect (2:13–14), as we discuss terrific points like being loved by Christ, being the firstfruits of the harvest, experiencing the work of the Spirit, and sharing the wondrous glory of Christ.

(2) The importance of standing firm for Christ (2:15–17), a topic dear to my heart as it concerns a deep love and awareness of biblical truth and theology. The prayer for comfort and strength (vv. 16–17) flows out of this, as knowledge of the word and of the truths encased in it provide comfort and give us strength as we face the vicissitudes of life.

(3) The place of prayer in our lives (3:1–5), as we discuss critical issues like the evangelism of the community (v. 1), the need for protection against evil and in particular against Satanic attacks (vv. 2–3), the faithfulness of Christ, who empowers us to live victoriously (vv. 3–4), and concluding with prayer as immersion in God's love and Christ's persevering presence (v. 5).

———

2. These two phrases use what is called a "subjective genitive," so that we translate them as "God loves us," and "Christ endures on our behalf" (God and Christ are the subjects of the verbal idea in each phrase).

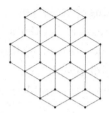

# DISRUPTIVE IDLERS AND CLOSING GREETINGS
### (3:6–18)

We don't really know much about this group Paul calls "the lazy idlers." We know they refused to work, that they made the people of the church take care of them and feed them, and that when they were castigated and commanded to take care of themselves they refused and were rebellious and disruptive. What we don't know is what their origins were. Two major theories have arisen. Many believe it was another result of the **eschatological** errors the church had made. A group believed the Lord was returning any day and thought if that were the case, the only important thing would be to get ready for his return. So they quit their jobs and went into prayer, fasting, and other things as they waited for the **parousia**. As one day flowed into another and Christ didn't come, they had to be fed and cared for, and the more "carnal" members of the church who still had jobs were forced to do so.

The other major theory flows out of the patron-client system that dominated the Roman world. The wealthy were expected to take care of the needs of those less fortunate, and clients owed their patrons loyalty and support on civil issues, giving them honor in society as benefactors of many. So this group decided that the patronage system was all they needed and refused to work, expecting the wealthy in the church like Jason (Acts 17:5–9) to supply all their needs. Paul then is saying they have gone too far and are misusing the system and contributing nothing to the church or the needy (making it clear that they are *not* the needy).

The problem is that while he discusses the solution to this indolent group, he never tells us its origin, and we simply cannot know which of these is correct, or if there is another reason for the group that no one has thought of yet. Of the two options, my personal preference is the eschatological one, for an entire group exploiting the patronage system like this just seems a bit far-fetched to me. Still, neither option is decisive, and we must admit we cannot know for certain.

The one thing we can know for sure is Paul's response and the model that this leaves for us when we face similar problems today. Let's explore how Paul handles this tricky issue.

## PAUL COMMANDS THEM TO ISOLATE
## THE PROBLEMATIC IDLERS (3:6)

We must remember from 1 Thessalonians 5:14 that Paul has tried to correct these lazy people before and get them to change their ways, but they have refused and in fact have been quite obstinate about it. Now he commands them "in the name of the Lord Jesus Christ." This is not just a personal issue or a church problem. The authority of the Lord of the universe is behind it. This command is from Christ, not just Paul or the church leaders. They are emissaries from the Triune Godhead in this. Moreover, it is a "command," not a mere request or suggestion. (One-third of all Paul's uses of the term occur in this passage.) It could not be more emphatic. The reason is to be found in the response of these listless, slothful ne'er-do-wells. They have been reprimanded several times and refused to listen or do anything. They have been lazy about their laziness! So it is time to get tough with them.

Note that Paul does not just address the command to the leaders. The entire congregation is involved. The pressure to obey and get right with the Lord must come from everyone in the church. Still, they are not yet excommunicated and cast out of the church, for they are addressed as "brothers and sisters," setting the stage for what Paul will say in verse 15: "do not regard them as an enemy, but warn them as you would a brother [NIV 'fellow believer']." Discipline in the church family must be loving, with the purpose not to punish but to redeem and bring about repentance.

The command is quite severe: "keep away from every believer who is idle and disruptive." The verb (*stellō*) is rare and basically means to "send one's self away" or "remain aloof." The NIV is a good rendering, and so this commands social ostracism. What Paul is saying in essence is, "If they don't want to contribute and do their part for the whole of the church, let them stay apart from the church." The reason is that they demand to be allowed to be "idle" (*ataktōs*), which means not just indolent but also "disruptive" or "disorderly" in their attitude and behavior. They are causing many problems for everyone else and have the church in an uproar.

Needless to say, with this conduct they are not living "according to the teaching you received from us," that is, "the traditions" they inherited from the church, a concept Paul used earlier in 2:15 when he told them to "hold fast to the traditions [NIV 'teachings'] we passed on to you," a command they obviously have completely disregarded. In this case these are official teachings about living in community as the body of Christ. He uses the concept of "receiving" these teachings, semi-technical language from 1 Corinthians 15:3–5 of truths "received" from the church and "passed on" to believers.

A text-critical problem should probably be addressed. The NIV follows what is called a "Western reading" (following B F G and others) by translating "*you* received from us," while the more likely reading is "they received" (with codices א A D and others). The KJV's "he received" is even less likely. With "they," the culpability of all the idlers is more strongly stressed. The guilty as well as the innocent have received these official church teachings and know them.

## PAUL PROVIDES A MODEL FOR A VIABLE WORK ETHIC (3:7-10)

### HIS EXAMPLE FOR WHAT NOT TO DO (3:7-8A)

Not trusting that they will simply follow what they are told, Paul wants to ground the command in a concrete model and chooses his own behavior among them. His purpose is to show why their refusal to work is so serious an offense by exemplifying the kind of conduct the church must be able to rely upon. He begins, "For you yourselves know how you ought to follow our example," with "ought," the Greek *dei*, speaking of absolute necessity.

Paul nearly always refused to accept support from the church for this very reason. He wished to supply an example of self-supporting work so he could not be accused of using his ministry for his own advantage. He wanted the Thessalonians to follow his model and work as hard as he did to take care of themselves and help others in the church. He had made this point in 1 Thessalonians 2:9 in order to show his concern for their needs, and once more he wants them to imitate his conduct (see 1 Thess 1:6; 2:14).

The area this time that they are to emulate concerns their work habits: "we were not idle when we were with you." It is one thing to tell people what the expected conduct must be, quite another thing to exemplify that conduct yourself. This is a lesson for us as well. Paul never made a point that he failed to follow himself. This is such an important point. We too often are making demands of our people that we fail to emulate in our lives. This is dishonest and hypocritical. We should always be aware of the necessity of living out what we are saying from the pulpit. Paul was able to point to his own work habits as an example to follow in living out the work ethic he was commanding.

He states his work ethic two ways for emphasis: "we were not idle when we were with you, nor did we eat anyone's food without paying for it." They worked hard for everything they had, and they never sought handouts. He is clearly separating himself from the despicable behavior of these lazy idlers. He is hardly saying it is wrong to go out to eat with someone who pays for the meal. This is a big-picture comment relating to a lifestyle of letting others pay for one's needs.

## His Example for What to Do (3:8b–9)

Our practice must always be to work and pay our own way, using the extra we accumulate to help the needy rather than to wait for others to help us. This is the point here: "we worked night and day, laboring and toiling so that we would not be a burden to any of you." The first half of this is also found in 1 Thessalonians 2:9, where Paul used it as an example of how much they cared for the Thessalonians. Here he gives another purpose: to provide "a model for you to imitate." There was a strategic purpose behind the hard work. Paul meant "night and day" not just metaphorically but literally. They likely did part of their leather work late in the day and at night so as to have the day time for mission work.

This was an incredible sacrifice and exhausting, but they felt they needed to do so to show the Thessalonians how important hard work was so as to do God's work properly (v. 9). The Thessalonians and especially the shiftless idlers need to mark this example and imitate it if they expect to please God at all. Paul begins, "We did this, not because we do not have the right to such help." This right for ministers to receive support while they minister so as to free them for full-time work on behalf of the church is found in 1 Corinthians 9:3-6: "the right to food and drink ... the right to not work for a living." Paul argues there that serving the church took all of one's time, and so this gave them the "right" to support in order to free them for this work. However, both in

1 Corinthians 9 and here Paul says he had decided not to exercise that right but to work to support himself.

The reason he gives here is "in order to offer ourselves as a model for you to imitate." There is both a negative and a positive aspect to this: in verse 8 the negative aspect is so they "would not be a burden," and here the positive aspect is so they would become an example to emulate. This latter is Paul's primary reason because it reflects on the idlers and addresses their problem. The emphasis on imitation frames the unit (vv. 7, 10) and provides the main point of the whole—the idlers need to imitate Paul's team if they wish to do God's will.

Note the progression of ideas. The section of verses 7-9 is framed by the necessity of imitating Paul's model (vv. 7, 9c) and the thought moves from the negative side (they were not idle and refused to take handouts) to the positive side (they worked night and day so as to burden no one and to be a model for others) of the same important point, the necessity of a positive work ethic.

## Paul's Teaching on the Issue (3:10)

Once more (see 1 Thess 2:9; 3:4; 4:1; 5:1-2; 2 Thess 2:5) Paul reminds them of previous teaching "when we were with you," as stated in Acts 17:1-9. They only had a brief time to train the new converts in the Christian life, but part of that training dealt with the Christian obligation to develop a good work ethic. It is possible that the problem of the idlers arose at a very early date (see also 3:6), and this principle at the start was addressing this troublesome situation.

Paul is reminding them of the principle developed earlier and taught often: "The one who is unwilling to work shall not eat." It is important to note that this does not obviate congregational care to the needy. These are not the needy; they are the indolent who refuse to work. It is clear that the problem is not an inability to find work but an unwillingness to look for work. Acts states clearly the principle for the truly hurting people in their midst: "They sold property and possessions to give to anyone who had need" (Acts 2:45); "they shared everything they had" (4:32); "there were no needy persons among them" (4:34); "from time to time those who owned land or houses sold them, brought the money from the sales and put it at the apostles' feet, and it was distributed to anyone who had need" (4:34–35).

Those who were not truly needy but instead truly lazy are in a different category. The congregation must let them taste the actual fruit of their "labor" and starve for a while. Paul will explain this further in the verses yet to come. They are in a completely different category and so are to be treated in a totally different manner. Christians work for two reasons: to take care of their own needs and not be a burden to others, and to have some extra resources to share with those who are less fortunate. Those who could work and simply refuse to do so are sinning against themselves, against God, and against those around them. So they must be isolated from the rest of the community and allowed to participate in the harvest they have created for themselves.

## PAUL EXHORTS THEM TO WORK IN A QUIET MANNER (3:11–12)

Paul has received a further report about these disruptive people: "we hear that some among you [continue to be] idle and disruptive." The problem is not being alleviated but is getting worse. This is likely a recent missive, sent since the first letter (1 Thess 4:11–12; 5:14) and updating the situation. We have no idea who either sent it or came to Paul personally (probably the latter since he says, "we hear"). Nor do we know how many had fallen into this error, only that "some" had done so. It was most likely several people at least, for Paul treats it as a major problem for the church. So this has continued for some time, possibly the entire time this church has existed.

He uses a well-written play on words to emphasize what they are doing: "They are not busy [*ergazomenous*]; they are busybodies [*periergazomenous*]." They should be working hard but instead are merely meddling in other people's affairs. Since they won't work and be useful, they have all this free time that they are using to snoop into other people's lives. The picture for today would be those who spend their days sitting on their front porch gossiping and prying into the lives of everyone around them. Upper-crust Romans had nothing but contempt for manual labor and refused to work with their hands. This is similar to the young widows in 1 Timothy 5:13 who have nothing better to do with their free time than "going about from house to house ... [and become] busybodies who talk nonsense, saying things they ought not to," probably gossip but possibly also indecent language.

Paul responds (v. 12), "Such people we command and urge in the Lord Jesus Christ to settle down and earn the food they eat." He addresses these people directly, probably expecting this to be read in all the churches (as in 1 Thess 5:27) and thus for this rebuke to be heard by the idlers. The two verbs appear in both letters, "command" in 1 Thessalonians 4:11; 2 Thessalonians 3:4, 6, 10; and "urge" in 1 Thessalonians 4:1, 10; 5:14; and they are combined here to give strong emphasis to the exhortation. The stress is on the authority behind the orders. It is not just the authority of the apostle Paul but even more that of the Lord Jesus. To ignore it is not just to act against the apostolic office but against the direct orders of Jesus, Lord of all.

"Settle down" is literally "work with quietness" and echoes 1 Thessalonians 4:11, "make it your ambition to lead a quiet life." It means to quit being disruptive and meddlesome in the lives of those around them. Instead, they should work hard, take part in the community life of their congregation, and "earn the food they eat." This picks up language from preceding verses, saying "nor did we eat anyone's food without paying for it" (v. 8), and "the one who is unwilling to work shall not eat" (v. 10). There are two commands here—get to work, and do so without fanfare and disorderly conduct.

## PAUL GIVES CLOSING COMMANDS (3:13–15)

### CONTINUE DOING GOOD (3:13)

Paul applies all that he has said to his readers by beginning, "As for you, brothers and sisters" (*hymeis adelphoi*). There is a direct separation of them from the idlers, who by their poor behavior have removed themselves from the family of God there. These disruptive people are not acting like true members of the community. The faithful, however, should "never tire of doing what is good." The verb means "do not grow weary," but Paul uses it metaphorically for those who refuse to stop doing good. It must be a constant in their lives. It also means, "don't let yourselves be discouraged" or "lose heart" in doing good. They must never give up, and good deeds must always be their characteristic behavior.

What Paul has in mind is helping the needy, as in Ephesians 4:28, where Paul commands the saints to "work, doing something useful with their own hands, that they may have something to share with those in need." The work ethic in the early church concerned not the accumulation of possessions (as it wrongly does today) but the ability to "do good" for the sake of the needy. There is a double thrust, doing good in general along with specific acts of charity toward the poor.

### OSTRACIZE THOSE WHO DISOBEY (3:14)

On the basis of the history of the Thessalonian church thus far, Paul could be fairly sure that the majority of the idlers would not respond well to this latest rebuke and would refuse to obey what he has said. They have followed the chain of church discipline laid out in Matthew 18:15–18, with at least three warnings presented in increasing severity, ending with the recalcitrant being treated "as you would a pagan or a tax collector." These idlers have virtually gotten to that point, so Paul states that the church should "take special note of anyone who does not obey our instruction in this letter. Do not associate with them, in order that they may feel ashamed."

That adamant refusal to listen to the admonitions of Paul or of the rest of the leaders of the church is the basis of the disorderly conduct that had done so much harm in their church. So it was time to take direct action and make "special note" of the disobedient. We do not know if this was a special list, but that is likely. By virtue of the rest of the command, all those who fit this rebellious category were to be noted, and the whole church was to be made aware of them.

The church would refuse to "associate with" these people, either socially or in the church. It is difficult to decide if this is the Jewish "ban" or Christian excommunication (compare Matt 18:17; Rom 16:17–19; 1 Cor 5:9–11; Titus 3:10–11; 2 John 10–11). It definitely repeats the command of verse 6 to "keep away" from these difficult people, but it does not seem to be intended as an excommunication, for there is no indication they are to be removed from the church rolls or considered to be apostate from Christianity. Most think, however, these people are to be restricted from participating in the worship services or in church social gatherings, and the people should stay away from them socially.

The purpose is to force them to feel the "shame" they have brought upon themselves. This was an honor-shame society, and so shame was a powerful deterrent. Everything in ancient life centered on community acceptance, and so social ostracism and community censure were a serious thing. This would provide strong motivation to conform. Also, it must be noted that the purpose of the ostracism was to get the person to repent, not to punish them. If they got right with the Lord and with the community, all would be forgiven, and they would be reinstated to the congregation. The goal is restoration to the community, as in Galatians 6:1: "If someone is caught in a sin, you who live by the Spirit should restore that person gently." Paul will develop the "gently" aspect in the next verse.

## Warn Them As Brothers and Sisters (3:15)

This discipline is to be firm but not harsh, and Paul wants to make certain that Christian love guides the entire process. So he exhorts them, "yet do not regard them as an enemy, but warn them as you would a fellow believer." There is always a danger when disciplining an errant member of the community of allowing animosity to gain control of the process. In fact, the term for "enemy," *echthros*, means to "hate" someone. Paul wants to make certain this doesn't happen, for the purpose is not vengeance or getting even but, as said above, restoration of the individual to being a valued member of the congregation once more.

The key is that when the faithful warn or admonish them, they do so as "brothers" in Christ (NIV "fellow believers"). The verb is *noutheteō*, used in 1 Thessalonians 5:12, 14, for admonishing this same group. Paul on several occasions stresses the loving nature of all such admonition, as in 1 Corinthians 4:14 ("warn you as my dear children") or 2 Timothy 2:25 ("Opponents must be gently instructed, in the hope that God will grant them repentance leading them to a knowledge of the truth"). They are in essence rebellious siblings and as such deserve both discipline and love.

## PAUL DELIVERS FINAL GREETINGS (3:16-18)

### The Peace Benediction (3:16a)

This is a common prayer for closing Paul's epistles (Rom 16:20; Phil 4:9; 1 Thess 5:23). Normally the prayer addresses "the God of peace," but only here does he write, "the Lord of peace." In addition he adds "himself," emphasizing the presence of Christ. ("Lord" in Paul's writings always refers to Christ.) Peace as designating a right relationship with God and the tranquility of soul it produces stems from the work of Christ and is ours on the basis of the authority of Christ. This may also echo the promise of peace in John 14:27: "Peace I leave with you; my peace I give unto you."

The Lord of peace is asked to give them "peace at all times and in every way." This probably looks back to the day of the Lord issue in 2:2 and the alarm many felt as a result of the false prophecy. They all now have peace regarding their ultimate future with "the Lord himself." This in a sense culminates the whole letter and all the difficulties it enumerates the Thessalonian church as experiencing. For instance, the Lord is watching over the severe persecution they are passing through and promising them "peace" in the midst of all their suffering. The phrase "at all times in every way" is comprehensive and means that in every single problem they encounter, Christ will be there for them. That is a wonderful promise to every one of us as well. My mantra has always been, "Do you want to hear of my trials? How long you have? Shall I list them alphabetically or topically? I have one for every occasion!" This says that in every single one of them Christ is there to watch over me and give me peace. Each one will work out for the good (Rom 8:28).

Peace is also critical in the difficult situation of the quarrelsome idlers in verses 6–15. As the church disciplines them and tries to wake them up and bring them to repentance, tumult in the church could easily be the result. Only Christ can bring peace out of the disruptive process, and that is Paul's prayer. Discipline in the church is the most difficult area of church life, but it is also one of the most important areas, for we all must maintain a strong Christian walk and please the Lord with our lives. Discipline is necessary for that.

## Prayer of Encouragement (3:16b)

The basis of that "peace" is found here, drawn from similar Jewish promises (Judg 6:12; 2 Chr 15:2). The peace of Christ is anchored in the presence of Christ: "The Lord be with all of you." The omnipresence of the Lord Christ with every single one of his followers is the very heart of the new depth of peace that is ours in a troubled world. This is the "Emmanuel" that lies at the very core of

Matthew's theology (Matt 1:23; 18:20; 28:20). In all the difficult situations early Christians saw themselves experiencing, the realization that the Lord of creation was with them at every moment
was critical (Acts 18:10; Rom 15:33; Phil 4:9; 2 Tim 4:22). When they
are being slandered, mocked, and mistreated at every turn by
their neighbors, and when life delivers them one hard blow after
another, they can bask in the presence of Christ in their midst and
know they are never alone.

### Personal Greeting with Autograph (3:17)

Paul, due to his extremely poor vision, could not write his letters himself but had to dictate them to an **amanuensis**, or secretary. In all his letters except Galatians, Ephesians, and 1 Timothy
he follows letter-writing custom by adding a personal greeting
and signature "in my own hand" at the close of the letter to prove
he is behind it. In Romans 16:22 he names Tertius as the amanuensis; here he does not tell who this person is. In 1 Peter 5:12 it is
Silas, part of the team here, and he may be the scribe here as well.

Paul then tells the reason why he is following this practice on
this occasion. He wants to add a "distinguishing mark" to authenticate the letter. The term is *sēmeion*, a "sign," meaning an authenticating sign that proves Paul was truly the author. We need to
remember the possibility that a false letter claiming to be written
by Paul caused so many problems in 2:2, so this would be an important mark. The "sign" was not just his signature but the whole sentence written in his own handwriting. It is likely that several of the
leaders could authenticate that the handwriting was Paul's. So he
adds that he uses this mark "in all my letters. This is how I write."
There may be a hint that they can go back to the false letter of 2:2
and see that this sign-mark is missing there.

### Closing Benediction (3:18)

This closing prayer is identical with 1 Thessalonians 5:28 but with
an added *pantes*, "with you *all*." He is emphasizing that divine

grace is available to all Christians, even to such as the idlers who are living in disobedience. In fact, they need God's grace most of all, for it alone can help them to repent and live so as to please God. These disorderly people are still the objects of grace and as in 3:15 should be considered brothers and sisters in the church. Grace has brought salvation to the Thessalonians, and it will take them to heaven to enjoy God's blessings for eternity. Grace and peace began this letter (1:2), and it is proper that grace and peace close the letter as well. This passage contains two relevant lessons for the church today. First, there is the question of dealing with people who refuse to work and cause major problems for the church and for charitable organizations. It is very important to differentiate them from the true needy who would like to work but are denied the opportunity. The principle is quite clear: those who refuse to take care of their needs should be denied access to help in order to wake them up and teach them the importance of taking care of themselves.

The second is the clear presentation of the Christian work ethic, seen especially in verses 7–10. First, we refuse to allow ourselves to be lazy and so work very hard to take care of our own needs. As a result we earn everything we receive in life. People will never have to provide for us because we provide for our own needs and earn our own way. On the positive side, our hard work has as its goal not only refusing to become a burden to others but also providing a model for others to follow. Every parent is a model for their children, but this is true in the church as well. Its leaders must exemplify that behavior that others will want to emulate.

The principle in verse 10 is very difficult to apply in the complex situations of our day—"the one who is unwilling to work shall not eat." In other words, charity should be withheld from the indolent. The hard part is determining whether a person is among the indolent or among the needy who deserve help. Most are in this latter category, and the church must work very hard to categorize the people who come to them or are pointed out to them very carefully. I am on the congregational committee of our church, and we take this very seriously indeed. When Paul says in verse 12 that they should "settle down" and earn their keep, that means that we are willing to help them find work and seek to get them out of their bad situation. We are as responsible as they are to turn things around in their lives.

In verse 13 the command to live for doing good has a further implication for our work ethic. The purpose of making money can never be allowed to be the accumulation of possessions. American consumerism is not biblical Christianity. If we want to do it God's way we will work hard in order to use our accumulated profit for the kingdom's sake and to help the needy in our midst. We gain it in order to give it away (Luke 16:9). Of course, we need balance in this, and it is not wrong to enjoy the financial blessings God gives us, but biblically the primary principle should always be helping others.

The command to disassociate themselves from the idlers is another very difficult and complex action to do well. Again, the purpose is not to kick them out of the church. Far from it. However, the goal to make them ashamed of what they have done and bring them to repentance and proper behavior must be achieved very carefully, for it would be easy to overdo the negative side. The key is to treat them as a rebellious family member and do it in love. The ostracism must be there, but it is tempered by the loving manner in which it is carried out.

———

The closings of letters are unfortunately too often left out of preaching plans as being too mundane to make a good sermon. This is not true in any way. I could see an entire sermon just on verse 16 and the plea for the Lord of peace to bring his peace into our lives. Every part of the discussion under that verse could provide valuable material for us in our daily lives. Peace in a troubled world such as ours is impossible without the Lord of peace in charge. So long as we try to shape life in our own strength the way we would like it to be, we will utterly fail.

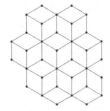

# GLOSSARY

**amanuensis** A scribe or secretary hired to write letters in the ancient world.

**apocalyptic** Refers to truths about God's plans for history that he has hidden in past generations but has revealed (the Greek *apokalypsis* means "unveiling") to his people. The name also describes a genre of ancient literature (including Revelation and parts of Daniel) that communicates these truths using vivid symbolism.

**chiasm (n.), chiastic (adj.)** Refers to a stylistic device used throughout Scripture that presents two sets of ideas in parallel to each other, with the order reversed in the second pair. Chiasms generally are used to emphasize the element or elements in the middle of the pattern.

**eschatological (adj.), eschatology (n.)** Refers to the last things or the end times. Within this broad category, biblical scholars and theologians have identified more specific concepts. For instance, "realized eschatology" emphasizes the present work of Christ in the world as he prepares for the end of history. In "inaugurated eschatology," the last days have already begun but have not yet been consummated at the return of Christ.

**gnostic (n., adj.), Gnosticism (n.)** Refers to special knowledge (Greek: *gnōsis*) as the basis of salvation. As a result of this heretical teaching, which developed in several forms in the early centuries AD, many gnostics held a negative view of the physical world.

**Hellenistic (adj.)** Relates to the spread of Greek culture in the Mediterranean world after the conquests of Alexander the Great (356–323 BC).

**paraenesis (n.), paraenetic (adj.)** Moral advice that deals with practical living. The term comes from the Greek word meaning "exhortation" or "urging."

**parousia** Greek for "presence" or "arrival," referring to the visible second coming of Christ.

**Shekinah** A word derived from the Hebrew *shakan* ("to dwell"), used to describe God's personal presence taking the form of a cloud, often in the context of the tabernacle or temple (e.g., Exod 40:38; Num 9:15; 1 Kgs 8:10–11).

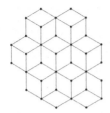

# BIBLIOGRAPHY

Beale, Greg K. *1–2 Thessalonians*. IVP New Testament Commentary. Downers Grove, IL: InterVarsity Press, 2003.

Best, Ernest. *The First and Second Epistles to the Thessalonians*. Black's New Testament Commentary. London: A&C Black, 1977.

Bruce, F. F. *1 & 2 Thessalonians*. Word Biblical Commentary. Waco, TX: Word, 1982.

Fee, Gordon D. *The First and Second Letters to the Thessalonians*. New International Commentary on the New Testament. Grand Rapids: Eerdmans, 2009.

Grant, James H. Jr. *1 & 2 Thessalonians: The Hope of Salvation*. Preaching the Word. Wheaton, IL: Crossway, 2011.

Marshall, I. Howard. *1 and 2 Thessalonians*. New Century Commentary. London: Marshall, Morgan and Scott, 1983.

Morris, Leon. *The First and Second Epistles to the Thessalonians*. New International Commentary on the New Testament. Grand Rapids: Eerdmans, 1959.

Shogren, Gary S. *1 & 2 Thessalonians*. Zondervan Exegetical Commentary on the New Testament. Grand Rapids: Zondervan, 2012.

Stott, John R. W. *The Message of Thessalonians: Preparing for the Coming King.* Bible Speaks Today. Downers Grove, IL: Inter-Varsity Press, 1994.

Wanamaker, Charles A. *The Epistles to the Thessalonians.* New International Greek Testament Commentary. Grand Rapids: Eerdmans, 1990.

Weima, Jeffrey A. D. *1–2 Thessalonians.* Baker Exegetical Commentary on the New Testament. Grand Rapids: Baker Academic, 2014.

Witherington, Ben III. *1 and 2 Thessalonians: A Socio-Rhetorical Commentary.* Grand Rapids: Eerdmans, 2006.

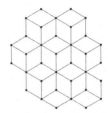

# SUBJECT AND AUTHOR INDEX

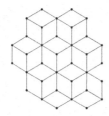

# INDEX OF SCRIPTURE AND OTHER ANCIENT LITERATURE

## Old Testament